No matter who you are, [your success] depends upon your effectiveness in meeting challenges. This is true whether you are a world leader, a performer, an athlete, a CEO, a copywriter, a soldier, a parent, a husband, a wife, or if you are on any of a myriad of other life paths at the moment.

If there could arise a new science by which our individual effectiveness could be reliably increased, a better human race could rise to meet the worldsize challenges mostly of our own making which now threaten our very survival.

This book is a test instrument. You have the opportunity to test whether it works for you or not. The measure is whether or not it increases your effectiveness. You will be the judge.

When you fall asleep, a part of your consciousness shuts down. The part of you that dreams (let's call it the Lower Mind) gets into situations that sometimes trouble you in the dream. If the part that is in charge when you are awake (let's call it the Middle Mind) were not shut down, it would have protected you from getting into those situations and from the bad feelings you felt in the dream.

Similarly, we hypothesize based on observations that there is another part (let's call it the Upper Mind) that is shut down a lot of the time you are awake, but the Upper Mind can be awakened by certain stimuli and your reaction to them. Each page in this test instrument (book) is designed to be such a stimulus.

When the Upper Mind, Middle Mind, and Lower Mind are all awake your faculties are at peak effectiveness and the things that you do — the solutions that you find — are characterized by an unusual level of creativity. At those times we say that you are in the Observer State. This name is used because when all of you is awake you have less of a compulsion to use words in your Middle Mind — and so you have the feeling that you are simply watching events in profound silence — without being emotionally captured by those events.

From this balanced place you are able to use all of your resources more creatively and effectively.

Even one page at random may be used for testing purposes. Others have found that even a random page a day increases effectiveness which has encouraged us to continue this line of research.

There are many portals or doors into the Observer State. Each of the twelve chapters uses a different doorway into the Observer State. Rather than just tell you about the state, the book gently brings you into the state.

Here's what each chapter helps you do, and the portal involved:

1. Reopen your mind to the existence of all possibilities.
   (DOOR: Suspend Certainty)

2. Drop acquired habits and mannerisms, and spontaneously express your true Self.
   (DOOR: Self-Observation)

3. Create unpredictable solutions to seemingly insoluble problems.
   (DOOR: Suspend Consistency)

4. Be real, rather than perform for other people.
   (DOOR: Suspend Rating)

5. Rediscover the unique experiment which Nature has designed in you.
   (DOOR: Inner Wants)

6 Perceive the profound web of cross-connections underlying every moment of present experience.
(Door: Outer Observation)

7 Develop the ability to concentrate at will in any situation.
(Door: Multi-stream Observation)

8 Learn not to become ruffled by time pressure, instead, relax into a previously unknown and remarkable grace.
(Door: Timing)

9 Realize the true role of the mind in the experience of the Self, and so have the mind serve you rather than vice versa.
(Door: Disidentification with Wordstream)

10 Know a greater inner clarity, and a greater receptivity to the inspired creative expression of your Self within.
(Door: Inner Observation)

11 Experience negative emotion as a brief creative stimulus, rather than remaining its victim.
(Door: Nonattachment)

12 Perceive Life from the point of view of All of It Combined.
(Door: Nobility)

# FREEING
# CREATIVE
# EFFECTIVENESS

*Doorways into the Upper Mind*

by

BILL HARVEY

THE HUMAN EFFECTIVENESS INSTITUTE

NEW PALTZ, NY

Fifth Edition, Copyright © 2002 by Bill Harvey
Fourth Edition, Copyright © 1982 by Bill Harvey
Third Edition, Copyright © 1980 by Bill Harvey
Second Edition, Copyright © 1978 by Bill Harvey
First Edition, Copyright © 1976* by Bill Harvey

*Originally published in June 1976 under the title
*MIND MAGIC: The Science of Microcosmology.*

All rights reserved.

For information write to:
The Human Effectiveness Institute
144A Mountain Rest Road
New Paltz, New York 12561
www.humaneffectivenessinstitute.org

ISBN 0-918538-04-1

Distributed by Bill Harvey Consulting, Inc.
www.billharveyconsulting.com

Designed and produced by Studio 31, Inc.
www.studio31.com


Printed in the United States of America

*Dedicated
to my bride and soulmate
Lalita Harvey*

Visualize the whole
universe as one thing

Every individual
of every species

Every idea
Every event
Every moment of time
Every percept
Every lump of matter
and energy

All parts of one thing

# Contents

FOREWORD TO THE FIFTH EDITION BY BILL HARVEY   XIII

### A THE HUMAN HERITAGE: WORD POLLUTION   1
*Because Words Are so Powerful, We Tend to Believe Them Rather than Assimilate Our Own Experiences.*

### B THE PRESENT: WORD POLLUTION OVERLOAD   19
*How the Tonnage of Words and Other Input Has Increased Past the Overload Point, Causing Hysterical Imitation in the Place of Real Life. Meditation as Accelerated Information-Processing.*

### 1 AVOID HASTY CLOSURE   45
*The Mechanism of "Making up One's Mind too Fast due to Overload Panic" and How to Avoid This.*

### 2 AWAKENING REAL WILL   59
*"Losing Oneself and Becoming a Rolebot" and How to Undo This.*

### 3 THE ORIGINALITY MOMENT   71
*Demechanizing Oneself by Broadening the Range of Creative Possibilities.*

### 4 SELF-RATING IS IRRELEVANT   87
*Relieving the Burden of Constant Self-Judgment.*

### 5 WHAT DO YOU WANT?   93
*Stripping Away Imposed Motivations, to Find out What "The Me That Was Born" Wants.*

### 6 OPENING THE SENSES   113
*Seeing More of What Is.*

7 STAYING FOCUSED THROUGH COMPLEXITY   127
*Effectively Dealing with Many Things at Once.*

8 "IN ACTION, WATCH THE TIMING"   137
— *Tao Te Ching* of Lao Tsu

9 DISIDENTIFYING WITH THE THOUGHT SENATE   153
*Not Throwing Your Authority Behind Untested Head Spewings.*

10 IMPROVING INNER VISIBILITY   173
*Allowing a Wider Range of Material Through the Interior Verbalizer.*

11 TRANSMUTING NEGATIVES INTO POSITIVES   191
*Turning Dilemma into Opportunity.*

12 VISUALIZING THE WHOLE UNIVERSE AS ONE THING   217
*Identifying With All You Perceive.*

PRACTICAL APPLICATION   235

OUTRODUCTION   255

INDEX   265

## Foreword

## Why the Book
## *Freeing Creative Effectiveness*
## Has an Effect

*And what makes it different from other books*

INITIALLY THE BOOK was a compilation of intuitions and thought patterns which with reasonable reliability led the writer to experience periods of verifiably higher effectiveness.

The writer, however, did not know *how* those stimuli caused or catalyzed effectiveness.

Learning how this causation happened was of interest.

So draft copies of this book were distributed with fall-out postcards in the back requesting reader feedback. An address in the back of the book invited letters. A lifetime moneyback guarantee was offered. All of these mechanisms invited feedback of some sort.

So far the stats are approximately:
35,000 books sold
2000 letters and cards received
11 books returned for refund

Initially this feedback did not point to a specific process by which the book had its effect. The letters and cards said that the book had positive life-changing effects that surprised the readers who were not used to getting such effects from a book. However the range of effects described was so broad that it did not provide any clues as to how the book actually worked. The few book returns came with little information.

Over time fortunately some patterns coalesced out of studying the results of hundreds of personal interviews with readers, the letters and cards, and all other available information. Here, for example, is what readers say about what makes the book different from other books on the same general subject:

- Experiential — it focuses on the intimate reality of what life is really like, looking out from inside a conscious self, and not knowing too much for certain about anything

- Empirical/Scientific/Verifiability — it does not ask you to take anything on faith, but to test certain things in your real world and note the effects

- Instructions You Can Follow — the language is not vague but explicit, clear and simple with no hidden assumptions about mutually-understood meanings of words

- Operational/Interactive — everything is designed to be put into practice

- Computer Software Metaphor — where ephemeral phenomena need to be verbalized, requiring some abstract construct or model, the one that is typically chosen is the by-now-familiar concept of computer software operating within our conscious biocomputer

- Eerily close to home — the book verbalizes things that go on inside all of us that usually never strike us as being worth verbalizing; sometimes one realizes that a page in the book is speaking to us something that we ourselves realized long ago to which we simply paid insufficient attention.

One specific example of how the book offers instructions that can be easily carried out, is with regard to the practice of meditation. Often in discussions of how to meditate one hears the words "First you must still the mind." This is not bad advice but just that those words alone do not automatically equip the meditator to achieve such stillness. In the book the instructions relate more to letting the mind do whatever it wants while *disowning* it. The latter type of instructions are more operational. They equip the user with a strategy that in the end achieves the stillness so difficult to achieve directly. (More experienced meditators can however go direct.)

What does meditation have to do with effectiveness? Meditation, we hypothesize, is a more efficient and effective processing mode. It is characterized by no delays putting things into words. Instead the mind gets the point of each thought while it is still an amorphous feeling-image packet, before the energy of translating it into words is expended. The intellect races ahead on an accelerated basis and everything in the database is apprehended simultaneously and in relative perspective. Wisdom is more likely to occur.

In fact the meditative state is what makes the book work. The book is a collection of stimuli that catalyze that state. The object of the book is not for the reader to experience that state only during sit-down meditation but in every moment. The sit-down meditation periods are enabling to the state coming on during periods of life action.

We believe that a more actionable, operational word for the state is the Observer state. This is another name for the meditative state. There are obviously many names for the state in many languages. Dr. Mihaly Czikszentmihalyi of the University of Chicago has given it the excellent name the Flow state. In show business it is universally known as being On. In the yogic tradition it is known as the Witness state.

The reason we choose the name Observer state is because our aim is to have the name itself have effect. To do so the name must remind the user of a way of getting into the state. The other words appear to us to have less functionality in that regard — except for the word Witness which works for us almost as well as Observer.

In the Observer state one has temporarily suspended preferences about outcomes. From this in an autonomic cascade one has also dropped the mantle of self-protectiveness and the accompanying Defender or egoic state, one has the inherent motivational/emotional strength to deal with any outcome ... and one is therefore simply observing. Since nothing is being rejected there is a merging of inner and outer. One's consciousness is creating the event and is the creation itself. These latter abstract ideas are not necessarily present as one is not focused on any ideas, but is in fact above words ... ideas are coming, leaving insight and then going out rapidly.

Observer triggers are woven through the book. Here are some of the more obvious examples from different chapters:

Page 64 — Observe yourself as if you are observing another entity.

Page 73 — Start your life anew with a clear slate each moment.

Page 90 — Do not constantly rate your success.

Page 102 — When you hear in your head the words "But I really want that!" you must identify who that "I" is.

Page 114–115 — Look at everything as if seeing it for the first time.

Page 134 — Look without talking to yourself about it but accept useful words which float up unbidden.

Page 137–138 — Do not move but observe yourself not complete the intended act.

Page 154 — Do not identify with your thoughts. You are not the thinker of the thoughts; you are the hearer of the thoughts.

Each chapter in fact is another strategy for triggering the Observer state. One chapter approaches this through the concept of timing, another through the concept of self-rating, and so on. The number of approaches is conceivably limitless. The book is a compilation of the stimuli which have worked best for the writer. They are offered for testing so that those which work for the individual may be retained and used, potentially leading the user to develop his or her own even more individually effective trigger stimuli.

Our work is motivated by the hypothesis that as more people are able to stay longer in the most effective state of consciousness all of the other problems of the world will tend to be solved by them.

We thank all those who have contributed to our work over the years — a list too large to acknowledge everyone by name. Special thanks go to those whose work has made an enduring impact on this book: Yana Lambert, Jim Wasserman, Jan Bertisch, Virginia DeLillo, Russ Norman, Lalita Harvey, and of course George and Christine Niver.

— BILL HARVEY
Mohonk Mountain
March 23, 2002

# A.

# THE HUMAN HERITAGE: WORD POLLUTION:

*Because words
Are so powerful,
We tend to believe them
Rather than assimilate our own experiences*

### Word-Intoxication

**All words hypnotize
to some extent.**

## *Where Did Words Come From?*

From the depths of our soul.

They were discovered *inside* us, not invented.

The evidence of similar-root-noises-for-similar concepts across separated peoples, attests to this.

We *all* discovered something like the noise *mama* for mother.

Even apes apparently make similar sounds
for the same concepts as we.


It is as if we were all discovering
the same MASTER LANGUAGE,
distorted into various different directions
by the effects of different
genetic/environmental conditions.

## Words Just Became Important Recently

We came down out of trees
over 1,000,000 generations ago.

For 999,750 of these,
humans used or heard
*only a few* words each day.

Over just the last 250 generations,
this has increased to *tens of thousands* of words
going through the average human head each day.

Note: "Generation" = 20 years.

## Words Have Tremendous Programming Power

Words are not arbitrary sounds we can choose to ignore.

They are tailored
by physical (pre-human interference) nature
to fit our sensoricognitive biochemistry.

Like a key in a lock:
words were *discovered from* inside of us.

They can be used by a talking head
to a separate listening or reading head,
and when they are so used,
they tend to exert a behavior-impacting influence
on the listening/reading head.

When the ancients talked about spell-casting,
it wasn't just their superstitious ignorance at work.

They were recognizing
the hypnotic power of communication,
lifted to a new level by the use of WORDS.

# How Do Words Compound the Power of Communication?

By making it far easier for conceptualization to occur.

*Conceptualization* is the structuring
of individual perception-items (percepts)
stored in memory,
into association-clusters
with specific "relationship bonds"
between percepts associated.

Like making a tinker-toy.

*Your* concept of freedom, for example,
is a tinker-toy of all of the specific words,
pictures and feelings you have stored inside,
associated with the retrieval-keyword "freedom".

Until words were popularized,
people tended not to build such elaborate tinker-toys
in their minds.

Associations among percepts
tended to cluster into "attraction" and "repulsion",
without many finer breakdowns.

This meant that we tended, when we wanted an effect,
to repeat *all* of the "causes"
which we associated with that effect.

This is undoubtedly how the program
of throwing salt over the shoulder,
the program of blessing people for sneezing,
and all other "magical" programs first arose:

they had happened in the "first instance"
and were thereafter regarded as causally essential.


Our magical phase preceded words
and was pushed out by words.


Words gave us the power
to more easily *separate* things into parts.
We didn't have to conceptualize
only with *wholes* any more.

We could put a word-label on a part of an event,
to more easily trace whether or not that part
*always* went along with the event or not.


Words appear to have kicked off a phase
of developing the *left* lobe of the cortex,
which handles data sequentially-analytically
rather than holistically.

When we were concentrating on our right-cortex,
we *were* able to achieve certain effects of persuasion,
"getting our way", etc.
we didn't understand at all —
but we knew they worked and we used them.

Childhood is a time through which
each of us has the opportunity
to re-experience the whole evolution of the race,
first-hand, in microcosm.

As children,
we do have "magical" means of getting our way
through gestures and moods that somehow work.

So the race has always wielded
a lot of right brain power it never understood.

Then it took up words,
wielding vast left brain power,
which the race also used with only faint understanding.

*As words can hypnotize*
*they can also de-hypnotize.*

*Out with the bad air*
*in with the good air.*

Man comes into the world.
He finds out certain things:
for example, he finds out that fire burns him.
This "finding out" we call *knowing*:

when someone has a true picture in his or her mind —
"true" meaning that the picture corresponds
to the external reality —
we call this *knowing*.

So if a man has a picture in his mind
of fire burning his hand,
we say that he knows that fire can burn him.


So far, language does not yet exist.
Man can know without language
by holding true images in his mind.
There is no "believing." "Believing" comes into the picture
when language is invented.

With language, one man who knows something
can pass on this knowledge to another man
who has not yet discovered it for himself.
The latter man,
in accepting the former's knowledge as true,
"believes" it.


As we all now know, this "believing" often leads
to the holding of untrue pictures in people's minds.


The cure is to cut down on believing —
tend to only hold pictures in one's mind
of the things one has seen oneself.

## *Belief Was Never Much of an Issue Before Words*

Belief = be lief = be for me.

I believe him = he be's for me on that.
                he was there.
                he saw it.
                he sees it for me.
                he sees it — I see him see it.

Cosmic humor: Most belief is founded on the form,
                     not the content,
                     of the words believed in.

## *Disidentifying with the Feeling of Belief*

At almost every instant you are likely to experience
the feeling about a given postulate:

"It is so."


Look for that feeling,
and when it arises remind yourself:

"It may not be so."


Be willing to act based on your judgment
as to whether something is more likely to be true
or to be not true;

but do not *believe* that it is
either true or not true.


In this way, belief is unnecessary to action.


Be especially wary of the feeling of belief
at times when you have a thought
and then do not contradict it.

Simply the experience of non-contradiction
suggests to the belief program
that it energize itself.

Thus, you must guard against the tendency
to believe any thought you generate.


This can best be done
by remembering to say to yourself (but not in words)

"It may not be so"

in response to every thought.

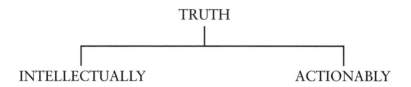

The definition of Truth at the intellectual level
is what can be made to sound reasonable
based on the words you use.
Intellectual reason can find some truth and some falsity
in every statement,
depending upon how it is interpreted.

The definition of Truth at the action level
is what works when you actually try it in reality ...
i.e., what the universe reinforces.

We need to make action decisions each second.

We need to make intellectual statements
a few times a day.

The two are usually unrelated.

Few people living in the Scientific Age
have realized that the Scientific Method
can be applied to Life ...

## *The Application of the Scientific Method to Personal Life*

In the usual unscientific approach to personal Life,
if someone gives you a piece of advice
you either believe it or disbelieve it.

In the scientific approach to personal Life, you neither
believe it nor disbelieve it.

What you might do is test it.


This also covers advice from "your own thoughts".
It even covers "advice" from "your own feelings".

In other words,
your own feelings might steer you right,
might steer you wrong —
you can't assume one or the other
because there have always been instances of both.

You can only "test" a particular feeling
by seeing its results:

    1. First in a *simulation* run in your head
       of what could happen
       if you were to "run with" this feeling;

    2. Then, possibly, by "going with" the feeling
       in *real Life*
       and *seeing* what the consequences *are*.


So it ALL boils down to:

Whose advice to follow?

There is the advice of the mind
        the advice of the heart
        the advice of the gut
        the advice from others
        the advice from books,
                memories,
                etc., etc.

The only way to know is to try experiments.

Be sure you remember which advice
you are testing at the moment,
so you know why you are getting certain results
(there is a tendency to forget).

*Example:*

Let's say somebody, maybe a parent of yours,
when you were small, said to you
"Hey — dig it — unselfish actions *pay back* better."

Let's say you had a flash of real understanding
and decided to try this advice.
You would have found that it *works*.

In trying this advice out in practice,
conscious of what you were doing
and willing to see the advice succeed or fail
in all objectivity,
you were living that moment
by the scientific method.

This is the way a "guru" lives each second.

Watching the evidence of experience very closely
(inner and outer experience)

Stepping back a pace from all the opinions.

## The Guru Has/Is Savoir-Faire

What impresses people about gurus?

They seem to know how to do everything right.

Like certain fictional heroes,
and people in history's favor.

This implies the existence
of a Best Operating Procedure
that they have discovered.

The thing about a guru
is that he/she is watching very closely.

This way, *he/she learns*.

A flash to the wise is sufficient.

## *This Is What Neurosis Is*

Neurosis is the mouse endlessly trying the dead end.

*Not learning.*

Living with unsatisfactory stuff
in one's Life permanently,
as if it inherently cannot be overcome.

## *Unlimited Willingness to Refine One's Position*

In the usual unscientific approach to Life
one attempts to get one's positions unshakably firm
as soon as possible,
and then defends against any changes to these positions
with demonic energy.


In the scientific approach to Life,
one is always eager to take one step further
in any particular analysis.

Thus one is always making provisional action decisions
for *this time, now;*
keeping an open mind about later;

*suspending belief and disbelief.*


One's positions, this way, gradually *evolve,*
based on day-to-day *learning from experience.*

Unfortunately, most of the Race has forgotten how to do this.

# B.

# THE PRESENT: WORD POLLUTION OVERLOAD:

*How the Tonnage of Words and Other Input Has Increased Past the Overload Point, Causing Hysterical Imitation in the Place of Real Life.*

*Meditation as Accelerated Information-Processing*

*Information Overload: A Cybernetic\* Explanation for the State of the World*

Over the last 15,000,000 years or so
we humans evolved a neuronic net
which we call a cerebral cortex.

We are still learning how to use this new facility,
and currently it is running amok and hypnotizing us,

due apparently to an overload of "question-producing"
sensory input per average second.

---

\*Cybernetic = from the Greek for "Helmsman." The Science of Guidance Systems, human or otherwise.

This overload appears to have been brought about
by the successive waves of media revolution,
which began with the printing press
and have reached tidal wave proportions
in today's television, radio, Internet,
magazines, newspapers, books, records,
outdoor signs, matchbook covers, movies, plays
and so on.


The world was *very different* 600 years ago.

We estimate that about *seven weeks' worth*
of sensory "question-producing" stimuli 600 years ago,
is what we now get *in a day* —

about *fifty times the pressure to learn and adapt.*


Just as an "Ice Age" appeared to stimulate humans
to discover "travel" and master fire,

this media revolution,
while it has paralyzed the brains of our leaders
as well as ourselves,
also appears to be a stimulus for humans —
to evolve *the capacity*
*to remain focused through complexity.*

## Cybernetically Contemplating the Brain

In order to appreciate how
"question-producing" sensory overload
can have such a powerful effect,
one must cybernetically contemplate the brain.

The neuronic net we call the cerebral cortex
contains about 13 billion neurons,
each of which is capable of relating
in many different ways*
to thousands of other neurons around it.

Let us visualize this as transparent,
as if it were a force field rather than matter,
so we can look *through* it in our minds.

When sensory input comes in,
it moves from neuron to neuron.

At each neuron, it encounters other information,
and in some cases,
the contact results in a cognitive association
between the new input and a memory.

Brain researchers can tell that the incoming sensory data
are "filtered"
(as if through a grid)

as it moves in through layers of neurons,
each of which check the data
from slightly different "viewpoints".

---

*Most neurons can either "fire" or "not fire". Some, called "microprocessors," have a wider repertoire. However, even the two-way neurons can have a *range* of meanings depending upon which other neurons are firing.

This is how the brain updates many of its files
based on each new piece of data passing through.

Something we see on the street
may trigger "notes to oneself"
in several different "files"
without our being consciously aware of all this
(because there is so much going on so fast
inside *and* outside).

Because of the many logical connections
between each bit of incoming sensory stimuli
and each bit we have already stored as memory,

a cyclopean computer update —
the kind that would daunt human computer specialists —

takes place in our brain
each second our eyes are open on anything
other than a totally familiar scene.


Yogis estimate that 70% of the energy we consume
is consumed through the eyes.

Today's Media Revolution proves that
what we let into our eyes and ears
is much more of a factor in our well-being
than what we let into our stomachs.

We have gotten used to treating
our precision electronic circuitry
most carelessly,
by feeding it sustained hyper-overload
with scarcely a letup.

As if our neuronic nets were more like Sherman tanks.

There's your brain there every moment
like a secretary tugging at your sleeve
asking you where to file something
and your answer requires a decision.

But meanwhile, outside your eyes —
the world still wants you to do this and that
(and it asks questions too!).

Before the Media Revolution,
people just took their time,
thought things through pretty carefully and slowly,
and worked out all the details.

Today there are *too many* details.

The brain shifts
into *a different kind of functioning entirely.*

The brain represses dissonance.

It accepts that questions needn't be answered.

And it lets itself regard certain questions
only long enough to identify them
as having been looked at before,
then it puts them away
with a "characteristic-habitual-decision-feeling"
as if the matter were solved . . .

We call this phenomenon "hasty closure".

In other words, we let ourselves fool ourselves
into ignoring things we should be understanding:

because we "simply haven't got time".

(Actually, we don't know where to begin.)

## A Different Kind of Functioning Entirely

When people are hypnotized by the things they are told,
their resulting emotional motivations
drive them at a hectic pace
precluding meditating on their own experience.


They "click into
EMERGENCY OVERSIMPLIFICATION PROCEDURE" —
another way humans can process information,
other than the way that is normally best.



In this EMERGENCY OVERSIMPLIFICATION PROCEDURE,
our biocomputers follow a grosser logic.

For one thing, in EOP,
everything must be either black or white.
And it must be decided immediately, based on precedent.

We also have little foresight in EOP.


In meditation, we can see
where things will lead years hence
and so avoid entanglements we won't want *then*.

The mind has little agility for this maneuver in EOP.

## *Too Many Variables*

"Too many variables" is another way of defining
the root cause of today's mass hysteria.

These variables are programmed into our lives,
by words and pictures and gestures etc.,
via people and media and nature.

600 years ago it was mostly just people and nature.
And fewer people contacts per day.

Why is the increased load of sensory messages
so devastating?

Because:

- We get attached to having our lives come out a certain way (sometimes we get programmed into these attachments). This sets up a "maze" for us to get through, i.e., what we have to do to get what we want.

- We have strong emotional charges connected to these attachments.

- The more messages we hear, the more complicated we make our maze — the more conditions we are trying to bring about at once.

- Everybody's mazes get tangled.

- Everything "uncopeable with" we ultimately hypnotize away.

## Unresolved Experiences

These tug at the mind.

It is an automatic secretary function
of the brain which does this.
These are items the brain recognizes as relevant to goals,
and about which it knows more clarity will be possible.

It holds these messages for us,
and gives us these messages in odd moments.


When these items first came in through the senses
they were "question-producing"
and achieved cortical recognition,
although not necessarily conscious cortical recognition.

This resulted in dissonance,
and the items were put on "hold".


Now, with the brain giving us
*six week's worth of messages each day*
needing clear meditation and learning
so that we can improve our progress through our maze,

we repress *all of* these messages.*

---

*Then, the messages begin to *accumulate*. This usually begins at about age 5 (when real learning virtually stops) and lasts until death.

We refuse to learn.
"We haven't got the time."

Instead, we persist in our fixed, programmed pattern:

this is *not* a *normal* condition,
but a *pandemic pathological rigid shock reaction*
*to today's information overload.*

# We Plan Empirical Studies to Confirm or Disconfirm that:

1. A sensory overload relative to meditation time (to assimilate those inputs) causes a shift in how information is processed: *different* (simplified) biocomputer logics.

2. By perpetuating robot repetition of conditioned programming, these simplified logics reduce free will, powers of observation, sensory sensitivity, and in other ways unnecessarily hamper one in achieving lasting satisfaction from Life.

3. The simplified logics are intended by Nature to be used in short bursts for coping with actual emergency threats to survival, i.e., they are an alarm reaction.

4. The pandemic problem today is the inability to turn off the ever constant alarm reaction.

5. The difficulty in functioning through this alarm reaction is that learning is suspended. Experiences which need to be assimilated are repressed.

6. Meditation is the most efficient method of assimilating human experience.*

---

* Specific instructions on how to meditate are included on pages 182–189, 140, 130–135, 113, 121–122, 124, 95, 100, 238–242

## *The Source of Tension*

Unresolved experiences cause tension.

This is the body's way of "alarm"-ing us,
so we figure out what's bothering us.


In a "natural" situation, we stop and meditate.


On today's sensory battlefield,
there's a general feeling that to stop is doom.
Part of this is the subconscious awareness
of how many messages are waiting inside,
and how tangled together it all is.

So we keep up the act as usual,
and wait for some outside force to maybe come along
and save us some day.


This leaves us with a lot of tension.
Taking it out of the body directly (by massage*, etc.)
is treating only the symptoms.
The tension will therefore always return.

"He can't relax — he's got so much on his mind."




* Highly recommended anyway.

## Clarity Removes Tension

Tension is an alarm system prodding us to do something
we are not noticing needs doing;

like pain, a warning device.


Tension is a clutching. A keeping-tight.

The mind does it first, then the body follows.

Tension in the body
mostly comes from tension in the mind,
e.g., therefore fear
makes us take up less space physically.


We find that when we really achieve clarity
on whatever has been bothering us,
the tension eases.
Then the choices are clear
and one chooses in the proper time.

It is clarity that turns off the alarm system "tension".

## "Meditation" as "Automatic Clearout Process"

The number of
"not-perfectly-familiar-so-as-to-be-invisible"
sensory impressions
falling on the individual per second,
determines how much unresolved experience
will be created by a culture.


Subtract out that culture's propensity for meditation
("putting the biocomputer on 'automatic clearout'")
which is the fastest process
for resolving unresolved experiences,

and what is left
is the weight of residual unresolved experiences.


In our culture,
the high sensory glut
and low incidence of meditation
creates such a backlog
of unresolved activity in the brain,
that these electronic "tensions held"
become a distracting screen,
and we go into a kind of hypnotic trance.

We handle the trivial moment-to-moment stuff,
and lose sight
of the highest long-range possibilities
of our lives.

## *Meditation Is the Assimilation of Information*

It does to sensory food
what the liver does to physical food.


Unassimilated food turns gangrenous.
So do unassimilated experiences.


In meditation, the mind unclutches;

super-efficiently,
experience is assimilated;
patterns are recognized;
action implications become clear.


The resulting clarity eliminates the tension
of unassimilated experiences
which caused the mind to clutch up
in the first place.

## Humans Exist by Processing Information

*That* information is our own inner and outer sensory experience,

including words we are told.

*All of this tends to program us,
if we don't process the information
in a certain way nature intended.*

*If we do process it the natural way,
we program ourselves.*

The natural way of processing
assumes a reasonable ratio of
input volume : meditation time.

In today's reality,
this ratio has become highly *un*reasonable:

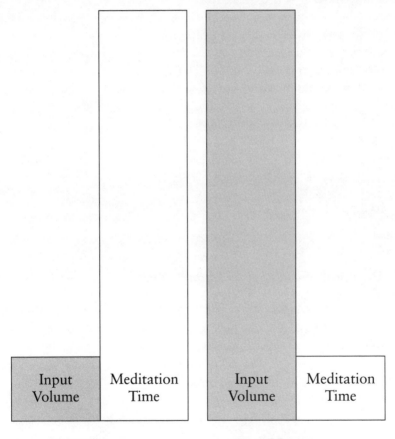

YESTERYEAR —
BEFORE THE
PRINTING PRESS

NOW —
MEDIA REVOLUTION/
INFORMATION OVERLOAD

## Assimilation = Higher Pattern Recognition

Picture a pyramid of many stories,
each one containing books ... a pyramid library.

The basic structure of any field of information
may be regarded cybernetically as a pyramid:*

This is how it is organized:

on the lowest floor (also the largest),
are the *specific detail* books,
covering diverse facts
from all of the fields of knowledge.

The books on the second floor
cover the same fields of knowledge,
but from a *"theoretical overview"* perspective.
We can imagine a whole rack of books on the first floor
telescoping upward
to a point in *one* book on the second floor.

The third floor *brings whole fields together.*

The fourth floor brings *everything* together
into *philosophic viewpoints.*

The fifth floor contains books written about
the *fundaments of philosophy* itself.

The sixth floor contains a single book.

In the capstone of the pyramid is a single word.

---

* With thanks to Fred Klein, 1973.

Each floor contains the same material as the floor below,
but in *integrated, reduced* form,
 i.e. from a higher, more universal perspective,
ignoring more and more of the "incidental details".

This pyramid model is to be applied
to any field of information.
It is possible for one's *perspective* to be on any floor,
or in the capstone.

However, this is not simply a matter
of *putting* one's perspective in the capstone.
It has to "float up", so to speak,
as a result of the assimilation process.

The many unresolved experiences in one's Life
need to be meditated on.
As a result of this process,
one gradually "floats upward"
out of "a lot of chaotic thoughts/feelings"
into a sense of *"everything falls into place"*.

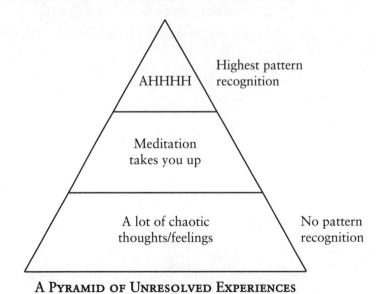

**A Pyramid of Unresolved Experiences**

## *We Are Involuntarily Shutting Down*
## *Our Inner and Outer Senses*
## *Against the Information Overload*

Most of our minds are on "hold".

The brain is holding many messages for you,
taking up much mindspace, mindenergy and mindtime
giving you these same messages repeatedly.
While with your conscious control over that same brain,
you repress and dodge these messages.

You haven't answered your messages in how many years?

There's a message for each person you haven't forgiven.
And for each pain in your body.
And for every other symbol
of something unresolved in your Life.
And for every question you've asked
that you're still not so sure about the answer to,
that is relevant to your "maze".

In effect, the brain knows
it has the information *you* need,
and it is trying to give it to you.

Meanwhile, a set of functions
often called the "subconscious" or "unconscious'
*gives you away*
in various social situations,
i.e. embarrasses you in various ways,
to get you to confront
some of these messages.


But we are not observant
because we are involuntarily shutting down
our inner and outer senses
against the sensory overload.

## *Skepticism Is the Anus of our Mind Clenching to Keep Out the Information Overload*

The severest human shortfall
caused by the information overload
is the limitation of possibility.

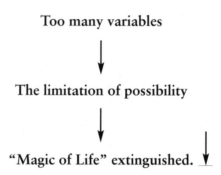

One of the most overwhelming surprises
one gets in deep meditation
is how complicated it really is
to figure out right action
in a typical everyday situation.

This is certainly the key subconscious deterrent
to really BEING: it is too complex now.

## We All Move too Fast

We pretend that we are capable of functioning
in this haze of complexity.

This is a hysterical reaction.

> What happens to most of us
> is that under pressure of time
> we take automatic positions on things,
> based on our programming.
> Without realizing it,
> most people are trying
> a desperate short-cutting approach to existence.
>
> We label this a hysterical "panic" reaction
> because it *continues to persist*
> *for a lifetime in most cases,*
> *although it proves itself unworkable*
> *every day.*

The realistic reaction belongs to the yogi under the tree.

> The yogi doesn't act on an idea
> until he has meditated out
> all of its possible connections
> to other ideas in his ken.
>
> Thus the actions never snag.

## Each Other's Windup Toys

All information
has some intrinsic command effect
upon the brain.
Even rhythms may be soothing,
or create a wide range of other moods.

Our brains are being washed in information
with some command effect over us,
from waking to sleep each day (and during sleep).


Ours is the Age of Background Brainwashing.


We don't even notice that it is there,
or why we buy those products
or snub those strangers.
How little of our behavior is under our own control;
how much was programmed from outside!

## We Become Shorthand Human Beings

There is always a subtle time pressure.
"Don't you dare waste my time!"
is the unspoken rule.

Thus, when someone asks a question,
we tend to flip back something that
"sounds like something we would say
in such a situation".
We usually give no fresh thought to the matter.

It is the automatic pilot.
Free will is switched off.
Creativity is a forgotten ideal.
The robot is playing its tapes.

This is the eventual result of a narrowing process
which takes place via communication exchanges
when we are very young.

We encounter such a large number of misunderstandings
(with many "iterations" to "unwind" each one)
that eventually we stop trying to *express*
what is inside of *us*,
and *content ourselves with flashing cliché signals
which everyone understands.*

## *The Capacity to Remain Focused Through Complexity Is a Key Survival Characteristic for Humans Today*

The point of *staying focused* is that it enables you to:

1. Catch more of the incoming stimuli;
2. Catch more of your own total reaction to these stimuli;
3. Identify the real priority items;
4. Simultaneously continue or change motor activity gracefully as needed;
5. Make decisions when needed —

*— without*
"distraction-resulting-in-only-partial-attention"
to *any* of these.

The true yogis
know how to do this.

Remaining focused through complexity
is a thing that can be learned
and trained.

# I.

## Avoid Hasty Closure:

*The Mechanism of "Making up One's Mind too Fast Due to Overload Panic" and How to Avoid This.*

Built into each human being
before birth
is an information-processing program

whose apparent purpose
is to make us need to understand
our external and internal experiences.

It works as follows:

certain experiences*
trigger a feeling of dissonance
in the mind;

you pay closer attention to and think about these
until you have a feeling
of having absorbed their information,

at which point
the feeling of dissonance goes away
and we say that you have achieved closure.

---

*Or "perceptions" or "percepts" (these words all used interchangeably).

*Hasty closure* can be defined
as those instances in which
it would have been useful to you
to think further before closure.


Not all percepts trigger dissonance,

but there are too many percepts available
relative to your Current capacity;


thus most external and internal percepts
are automatically screened out
by a process of instant closure
which avoids dissonance entirely.


For such percepts,
you are not even given
the opportunity to decide
how much thought they deserve;

they do not come to your conscious attention
and therefore
are given no conscious thought.


Obviously, whenever you achieve instant closure
by not even noticing a percept
which contains useful information for you,
this is also an instance of hasty closure.

Thus there are two types of hasty closure:

Type A: Instances in which you notice an object or a thought, think about it, reach your conclusions about it, and put it out of your mind too hastily.

Type B: Instances in which you do not even notice an object or a thought which contains useful information for you.

The types of percepts which will tend
to be screened out most frequently
by this second type of hasty closure
will be percepts
on which you have achieved closure in the past.

Thus as you experience more and more
different types of percepts,
fewer and fewer percepts will trigger dissonance;

you will stop looking at things you have seen before,
and you will stop thinking about things
you have reached conclusions about before.

In this respect the mind
acts as if there is never any need
to reopen old issues;

although relevant new information
may now be present in memory
with which to look at old issues from new angles.

Eventually one winds up
looking only at a narrow range of percepts
which are relevant to one's interests;

this tends to block potential change or expansion
of the individual's interests.

Know that percepts which do not trigger dissonance
and which therefore yield instant closure,
do so as follows:

Images of things that you have seen before
are stored in your memory.

When you are about to see something,
your mind automatically searches your memory
for a comparable object

(note the distinction between *you* seeing something
and *your mind* having already seen it).

If your mind finds something similar enough,
it projects the stored image
onto the new object
so that you do not ever see the new object,
but are merely dimly aware
that there is a familiar type of object there.

Dissonance is not triggered,
and this allows your attention freedom
to concentrate on remaining percepts
for which your mind
has not found a suitable match.

As a result of this,
you mostly do not perceive your environment,


instead perceiving mostly what you expect to perceive,
i.e., you usually see your mind's prediction.


Since most objects have more relevant detail
than you have ever noticed,
this process robs you
of the opportunity to add detail
to your image of most objects.


In some cases, the mental projection that you see
is significantly different
from the reality you do not see.


Example:

> You are in a hurry. You glance at a book title.
> You glance away quickly. A moment later you think,
> "'Fellow's Folly' is the name of that book; the same as
> a song I know; the author must also know that song."
> You glance back at the book title and read it carefully:
> "Free Four."

What has happened is that your visual system
was scanning for relevant clues,
since time did not permit larger sampling
of visual observations from each scanning sector.
It picked out the two words starting with an F.
After you looked away,
your mind experimented with alternate predictions,
based upon what you had
in your "F____F____" file drawer,
i.e., what memories you had of word-pairs
with initial F's on each word.
It then verbalized to you what seemed to it
to be an interesting prediction.
You looked back to test the prediction
and found that it had been a wrong one.

Another entity in your place
might not have looked back to test the prediction,
because as a result of even less attention
to head action,
that other entity would think that it *saw*
"Fellow's Folly"
and would have accepted the supposition
that the book's author named the book
after the song as established fact.

In this way, most entities "see the prediction"
and not the bulk of the reality around them,
in a continuous stream of such incidents
as described above.

*Society Increases the Tendency*

*Towards Hasty Closure by:*

*Creating Time Pressures,*

*Communicating Expectations,*

*Causing Negative Emotion,*

*Encouraging Black and White Positions,*

*And Valuing Sophistication*

## *Creating Time Pressures:*

You have to some extent
been programmed by the expectations of others.
Most of your actions have been expected of you,
and you have engaged in some of them
for this reason only.


At birth, you confronted an organized group of others
who taught you that you had been created
to fill a slot in their organization
(your current society);
for your most receptive early period,
you probably met no one
who was not in this organization.

Thus, you may be now spending most of your time
working for this organization.

Under such conditions,
your capacity for attention to matters
not strictly organizational is severely reduced.

Under such conditions,
your closure goal is intensified;
you cannot tolerate dissonance
which distracts you from the organization's tasks.
If you are also trying to spend some time
on non-organizational goals,
you may also regard dissonance
as distracting you from these latter goals.

Thus, you will strive for closure too strongly,
and achieve it hastily on many occasions.

This is the result
of the organization's infringement on your time.

## *Communicating Expectations:*

You are vulnerable
to being given expectations by other people.

Their communications to you
tell you what to expect
so that when you confront a particular reality
you may not perceive it,
instead perceiving
the expectation that was set up in you
by communications from others.


Most of your value reactions
have probably been conditioned in this way;

when you see something that you were told is bad,
you see its bad points:
how else, in fact, could you see so many things as bad
which have never hurt you?

This is not just a matter
of your attitude
when confronting an object;

it is largely a matter of your perceptions themselves:

you actually see something different
based on having received prior communication
about an object.


*In this way, society communicates expectations to you
which you then see
in place of seeing the realities themselves.*

## *Causing Negative Emotion:*

You have probably experienced
excessive negative emotion
as a result of worrying
about what others expect of you and think of you.

This is because our culture assumes
each individual to be
"valueless until proven otherwise".

As a result,
you have reduced tolerance
for the mild unpleasantness of dissonance,

and strive too strongly to replace it
with a feeling of
"It's all right",


thereby inappropriately hastening closure.

## *Encouraging Black and White Positions:*

Such positions are the result
of the oversimplifying effect of language
within the context of time pressure.


Under pressure of time
and under a barrage of communications,
you have taken excessively strong positions
on most issues,
despite the lack of sufficient objective evidence
justifying such positions.

Having taken such strong positions,
you will tend to be hasty in retaking them
and in screening out
or misinterpreting opposing evidence.


Your *expectations of reality*
*then program your perceptions,*
*causing you to receive only those visual*
*and other sensory images*
*which confirm your expectations about reality.*

## *Valuing Sophistication:*

An individual alone will tend to think;
an individual in society will tend to talk.

Talking is an expression of the inborn urge to think,
as it manifests itself in a social mode.

Those who think rather than talk
tend to be regarded as not cooperating with society;

this encourages talking and discourages thinking.


Whereas thinking progresses through falsehood to truth,
discarding the interim products of falsehood,

talking progresses through falsehood to truth,
retaining the interim products of falsehood.

Thus many heads are filled with falsehood,
generated by the process of talking,
and these falsehoods are repeated in later talking.


Talking is not usually motivated by the search for truth,
but rather by the search for approval;

thus approval is given
to those who say something already believed,
to those who say something interesting,
and to those who say something well,

but not necessarily to those who speak truth.

Given the welter of words one is forced to hear,
one soon tires of hearing
the types of statements which crop up frequently;

thus one learns to avoid
tiresomely discussing the simple and obvious,
and instead seeks approval
by discussing the complex and abstract.


Thus ignored, the obvious ceases to be obvious;
one's focus shifts from the obvious reality
to the abstract word.
One sees less and less of the obvious reality
as one spends more and more time seeking approval
by offering the new word.

One is motivated to believe strongly
in the truth of one's own thoughts,
so that these may be communicated to others
and approval received;

this acts as an impetus to closure
by demotivating one
from criticism of one's own thoughts.

As one is motivated
not to say that which has been said before,
one becomes motivated
not to look at that which one has seen before.


*Society's demand that one say something interesting
increases the individual's tendency
to screen out the familiar.*

# 2.
# DE-ROBOTIZING YOUR FREE WILL:

*"Losing Oneself and Becoming a Rolebot"*
*And How to Undo This*

## *People Run on Programs*

Programs are action patterns.

The way you get out of bed in the morning
is an action pattern.

Observe how you do it
for a few days in a row
and you'll see that pattern.

The way you throw off the covers,
swing your feet to the floor,
the way your body feels,
the things you think about,
your mood, people you think about,
emotions that strike you,
your attitude as you stand up — etcetera.


All of this is an action pattern.
Everything is not exactly identical from day to day
but everything is in a relatively narrow range
of variation.

This is because there are now sets
of interlacing programs
in your biocomputer upstairs.
They bring you through this action pattern daily
without your having to consciously think
about each move.


These automatic programs run 99% of your life.

## *Of Course, We all Override The Automatic Pilot at Times*

Such as when some potential danger
snaps us to full alertness,
and we don't make a move
without thinking about it first.

Such as when we are able to rise above
"automatic-pilot" anger.

Such as at moments of "peak realization"
or "expanded consciousness" or "satori".


But most of the rest of the time,
although we repress knowledge of the fact religiously,
we have no free will in what we do,

because the body's and mind's movements
are along conditioned paths
from which deviation is improbable.

*We always react to the same types of situations*
*in the same ways.*
*The programs are going through their steps*
*while we sleepily look on, along for the ride.*

## *We Consciously Participated In Creating these Programs*

Some of the "automatic-pilot"
program-punchcards in our head
were keypunched by our "conscious-mind-pilot".

Such as when you discovered how well you looked
smiling that way
and decided offhandedly to keep doing it *that* way
(at least at *those* times).
Then your "conscious-mind-pilot" forgot about it.

Your "automatic-pilot" does it faithfully to this day,
whenever *those* times come up.


*Good* "automatic-pilot"!


On the other hand,
the great preponderance
of our "automatic-pilot" programming
appears to be of the Pavlovian variety,
whereby we were addicted as we grew up
to certain types of shallow rewards,
without this being *anyone's* conscious intention.

## *Edit Your Head Tapes*

You have been programmed.

Every experience you have ever had,
every communication you have ever received
has implanted in you
the predisposition to act in certain ways
and to think in certain ways.

There currently are a large number of programs
operating in your head,
most of which you are no longer aware of
or were never aware of.

These programs interact
to determine precisely how you will behave
in a specific set of circumstances.

To the extent that you allow this to continue,
your behavior will be predictable
based on knowledge of your programming;
thus you will be a mechanical slave,
your life the mathematical resultant
of all your programming inputs.

It is, however, possible
to gradually become aware
of all of your programming;

to select which programming to keep,
which to modify,
and which to remove;

and to act with conscious awareness
of one's relevant programming
so as to be able to either ratify
or override it
in any given set of circumstances.


When these things are done,
one is no longer a mechanical slave
to one's programming
and can choose
when to use
each of his/her specific programs.


The first step
is to become aware
of one's own programming:

this requires close observation.

You must observe yourself
as if you are observing another entity
you have never known before,

Every word,

every tone of voice,

every minute gesture,

every action,

every thought

must be scrutinized from the standpoint of:

> Why was that done?
> What are the roots of such behavior?
> What is the motivation?
>
> **When might it have been implanted
> and by whom or what?**

You will find that the great bulk of your actions
serve petty ends
of which you cannot consciously approve;

for example, you will find that most of your words,
gestures and postures
can only be explained as role-playing mimicry
designed to allow you to feel
**approved-of.**

You will find
that even when you can do without outside approval,
you are still seeking inside approval
from other entities
whose viewpoints you have stored inside your head.

When you have stripped away all of such programming
you will no longer
be addicted to the support of others:

you will be taking what you consider
to be the best action
you know how to take at any given moment,
assessing the results of such action,
and revising future plans accordingly;

you will see **status** in society
as a form of scrip*
slaves are permitted to give themselves
in return for obedience.


**Strive to observe yourself more and more closely.**


For each manifestation, ask yourself why you did it,
and trace the causes back as far as you can.


Decide whether or not
you want to give rise to such a manifestation again,
in light of your goals.

If you do not want to, resolve not to.


However, make a prediction
in light of your past experience
with controlling yourself,
as to how successful you are likely to be
in suppressing such manifestations.

Thus, set a realistic goal
for reducing unwanted manifestations gradually,
rather than resolving to do the impossible all at once,
which would merely result
in discouragement and weakened self-belief.




*Scrip = ersatz money as given to Black American slaves by the "company" for use in the "company store."

If you always resolve to do something
you think you can do
although it is a little better
than you have done in the past,
you will gradually build self-belief,
permitting you to confidently
raise your sights a little more each time.


The effect of this process
is to telescope the delay between action
and thought,
so that at first you will find yourself realizing
soon after an inappropriate action,
that the action was inappropriate,
and why it was inappropriate;

then you will realize these things instantly after action;

then you will catch yourself in mid-action;

and then you will catch yourself before action.


(Actually, these four types of experiences
will always continue to occur,
but the latter types will become more frequent
and the former types will become less frequent.)


Some of the programs you will decide to remove
are programs which you once consciously established
and which were useful to you at the time;
but which have long since become counterproductive
based on changing circumstances
and your own increased capabilities.

It is an inherent characteristic
of any developing system
that heroes emerge
and are heroes — only in the context
which stimulated their creation;

as these heroes overcome and change such contexts,
the heroes themselves become the context to be changed.

Thus both coping systems and governments
begin as useful
and gradually become counterproductive;
this is the nature of the evolutionary process itself.

However, any system tends to be self-perpetuating:
programs may be visualized
as power centers in your head,
trying to survive despite their vestigiality.
Thus, they will get some senators\*
to speak in their favor;
and in honoring them for their past service,
you will hesitate to remove them.

---

\*Senators = minipersonalities that have been implanted in you by the internalized influence of others ... at least two from Mom (her Mom and Dad); at least two from Dad (his Mom and Dad); etc. Each Senator is a "parasite circuit" capable of "taking over your mind" by making you think *its* suggestions are *yours*.

## *Guiltless Housecleaning*

To compensate for these tendencies,
constantly review your own favorite programs
for possible vestigiality.
But in light of their past service,
do not blame any program for being counterproductive
as you remove it.

Housecleaning should be guiltless.


You will remove a program
as it no longer fits your developing gestalt;

up until that point,
the program fit
and you and the program
were not to be blamed for your union.


Avoid the temptation to be harsh
with the programs you remove;
look upon them not as enemies but as
"mischief programs";
they were necessary stepping-stones
to get to where you are now;

love them for this
while defusing their power over you for upcoming phases.

*As you remove your extraneous programming*

*you will be simplifying the number of variables*

*impinging upon any set of circumstances;*

*thus you will solve the circumstances for best action*

*more quickly and accurately.*

*In attempting to identify*
*your own unconscious programming,*

*be prepared for the pervasive to be invisible:*

*that which you do most continuously*
*will be hardest for you to detect and analyze.*

# 3.
# DE-ENERGIZING THE CONSISTENCY PROGRAM:

*Demechanizing Oneself by Broadening
The Range of Creative Possibilities*

The consistency program in your head
is concerned with maintaining
the apparent internal consistency
of all of your thoughts and actions.

In this endeavor,
it will naturally come into conflict
with your changing behavior patterns,
i.e., with learning.

It will seek to keep you
making the same mistakes in the same ways
so as not to reveal the past mistakes
for what they now seem to be.

However, your past actions were justified
by what you believed at the time;
no one ever takes a wrong action on purpose.


Your inconsistency over time
in no way reduces the net value of the universe;
seek to convince your consistency program of this fact.

If you find yourself "out on a limb"
doing something
you are no longer fully comfortable with,
it may be
that this is the result of your consistency program;

stop what you are doing
and reconsider all alternatives.


Do not do anything merely for the sake of consistency.

The tendency to be consistent
is born out of the implicit assumption
that if you have no preference which way to act
in a given circumstance,
the most logical thing to do
is to act in a way you have acted before.

While this assumption may appear logical,
its effect is to give power to precedent.


This is undesirable, since:
It limits experimentation and exploration.
Much precedent has been established casually.


As we proceed largely by trial and error,
much precedent represents error
and as such should certainly not be institutionalized.

Action so as to be consistent with precedent
reinforces the precedent,
developing it into a habit or programmatic addiction.
Programmatic addiction
"freezes" the entity into stasis
halting the evolutionary march of becoming.

The entity should ideally retain all power
over current behavior;
none should be yielded to the past or to others.

Acting consistent with precedent
is a form of hasty closure
and as such minimizes fresh thought,
reducing the potential for understanding.


Therefore:

Learn to identify which of your thoughts and actions
are inspired by your consistency program;

and subject these thoughts and actions
to objective critical review
as if the past did not exist,
and therefore as if no precedent exists.


*Start your life anew with a clear slate each moment.*


Spontaneously think and act
so as to break established patterns
of thought and behavior,

unless in a given instance
there are valid reasons for not doing so.

**Be aware of your power to change yourself.**


It is common for individuals
to focus on their past performance
as being predictive of how they will act in the future,
*regardless of their contrary resolutions.*

This is because there is *no feeling* of change inside
when a resolution is made;
thus one feels instinctively
that the resolution has not changed anything,
and thus will not change anything.


Since one has no confidence in one's resolutions,
they then have no effect;

then one says to oneself:
"I told you so!"
and continues to behave as in the past
with less hope than ever
of willing and effecting change.

**Resolutions, therefore, must not be made lightly,
for their non-effect will weaken the effectiveness
of future resolutions.**

Only resolve to do
that which you are determined to do,
after considering all aspects of an issue;

then let nothing stop you
unless and until your mind is changed
by new inputs and resolutions.


Be aware that you will not feel anything inside
when you make a resolution to change;

therefore do not expect to feel anything inside,
and do not take the absence of such a feeling
to be evidence that you are not any different.


You are different:
you have the invisible determination to act differently;
and you have total invisible power
to carry out this determination.

Be aware that the determination and the power
may be invisible,
yet real.

You can help prove this to yourself
by acting immediately on your resolutions,
even if the situation only allows this
to be done in small ways:
this will prove that you are now different
and will make your invisible will visible.

**Avoid describing yourself in unqualified terms.**

**Telling yourself or someone else
that you are a particular way
tends to make you more that way,
thus limiting your freedom
to create who you are at any given moment.**

If you believe that you are a certain way
as a result of your past experiences,
you are giving your past experiences power
to dictate who you are.

If you see how you have been influenced in the past
by your experiences,
this recognition in itself
is sufficient to free you
of the effects of experience;

*start anew that moment.*

Treat each second as the first second of your life;
and potentially as the last second.

When you hear yourself describing yourself,
say: "That's how I was.

How do I wish to be from now on?"

Predict and eschew
the predictable culture-conditioned response.

Do not always get angry in situations
in which anger is expected of you;

do not always contradict in situations
in which contradiction is expected of you;

do not always agree in situations
in which agreement is expected of you;


*avoid predictability*
*except where it is necessary*
*for the good of the universe.*


                              When you have an impulse
                        to take some minor familiar action,

                                  take some other action

                just to break the continuity of the program,
                                  and see what happens.

                                    This is a way of testing
                the continuing utility of existing programs;

                              it is obviously inappropriate
                in situations where it would introduce risk
                        of loss of value to the universe.

*Avoid mimicry.*

*You don't have to be like your friend
in order to be his or her friend.*


Do not submit to the prevailing worldview.

You may often be in the company
of a group of individuals with a common worldview;
this creates a powerful impetus
for you to fall prey to their worldview
without even realizing it.

They may value material success,
or wittiness in a specific vernacular,
or specific types of appearance and customs,
and so on;

and you may find yourself
accepting their negative judgment of you
against their standards.


This will be first manifested to you
in a tightening up of free self-expression,
formless negative emotion,
and perhaps even mild forms of mimicry on your part.


Remind yourself
that your worldview differs from theirs
and that yours is the only one which you submit to.

Prepare to and accept rejection from them
with equanimity.

Be honest with them
for they have no power over you;
no one has any power over you
because you are independent
of even what is done to your body;
it is not you;
you are inaccessible to any but yourself.

See if you and they can derive anything useful
from this confrontation between worldviews,
but do not seek to establish yours as superior.

Gently ask relevant questions and answer theirs;
otherwise do not expostulate.
Too much cannot be communicated in a single meeting.

Accept the contact assignment
which the universe has given you
as having good potential purpose;
see what happens.

Do not internalize their statements;
do not identify with their worldview;
do not accept judgment nor care about irrelevancies.


Consider no viewpoint sacred,
not even ours; not even your own.

*Objectively seek truth and value.*

Do not let yourself be carried off
by the momentum of others.

Others anxious to have something be a certain way
carry psychic momentum
which can be imparted to you
without your even realizing it.

Do not stampede in your predisposition to help;
give yourself a chance to think better of it.

What others *think* they want from you
may not get them what they *really* want.

Do not be influenced by the expectation
that they will misread your hesitation as not caring;

such influence makes you a slave.

Once you let yourself be moved by their momentum,
you may not later realize that this is happening,
for momentum interferes with observation.

Thus, be transparent to momentum from the outset.

When you look at something, see only what is there.

If it is an object which someone has created,
do not say to yourself "It is not well done";

this merely means
"It is not done in the way
usually said to be well done."


Our expectations create a perceptual screen;
*remove the screen by having no expectations
of what you are looking at.*

Allow yourself to see
what the creator of the object saw,
rather than comparing the object to any other.


As we grow older,
we are told that object after object is not beautiful;
we see fewer and fewer objects as beautiful;
fewer and fewer percepts entrance us.

We are looking at things through the eyes of others,
accepting what they have told us
about what is and is not beautiful.
We are comparing each created object
with other past created objects
which we were told were or were not well done.

In fact, every object is art,
every object can be appreciated,
but only if looked at without expectations.

Accept art criticism as art-in-itself
and ignore it as art-criticism-per-se.

*Ignore usual concepts*

*Of what is beautiful or ugly.*

*See what is really out there.*

*It was all put there by the same Artist.*

Implications:

Do not look at a situation and say that it is dull;

ask yourself instead
who do you know
who would consider the situation dull?

These are the people
who have programmed you
to look at this situation as dull.

Then ask yourself
what is to be learned from this situation;

when you find the answer,
dullness will turn to luster.

Do not look away from an object,
saying that you have seen such things before;

close your eyes and attempt to recreate the object
in complete detail.

Could you draw a detailed sketch of the object?


If not, you obviously retain only a hazy image of it,
not such a precise one as you suppose;
there is information there
which you have not yet gleaned.


Look at objects so as to be able to reproduce them,
not merely recognize them again.
Ask yourself why they are shaped
precisely the way they are;
there are reasons.

**This is information your senses can bring you**
**if you let them.**

Do not look at a situation and say that it is bad;

ask yourself instead
*how might good be brought out of such a situation;*

find that angle and grasp it;
actualize the good that is latent there
as much as possible.

In retrospect, you may laugh at the memory
of thinking the situation bad.


Bad things have such potential good wakes
it is difficult to maintain the position
that there are any bad things.


Let yourself enjoy simple things
rather than always demanding more complex ones.


Concentration on an apparently simple thing
will reveal it to have more complexity
than was at first apparent.

Concentration is the variable which reveals
that the simple-complex variable is an illusion.


Therefore, do not say that a substance is tasteless;
strive to experience its subtler taste.


Apply this rule to all of your senses,
no matter how numerous or few.

Visualize your feelings
as chords played on a multiplex organ.


This musical instrument has more chords to be enjoyed
than merely one
(happiness).


Therefore learn to enjoy all of its chords,

even those which the unenlightened might deem
dissonant and agonizing.


Continue asking the questions
you have never succeeded
in getting any kind of satisfactory answers to.


You and the universe are in a process of change

which will gradually
make some of these questions answerable.

You may find that if you ask yourself a question
which you long ago gave up asking,

you may *now* have some data in the files
which will cast some light on possible answers.

# 4.
# SELF-RATING IS IRRELEVANT:

*Relieving the Burden of Constant Self-Judgment*


Know that you are conditioned to rate yourself.

At any given moment in time
your self-rating program
is communicating one of two possible messages:
"(Your name) good boy/girl" or
"(Your name) bad boy/girl".

These messages are also emphasized to varying degrees.
All other self-evaluative statements
reduce to one of these two basic ones.

This self-rating program
is another internalized voice
which originally belonged to other individuals
who used it as a reward-punishment device
to condition you to perform in the ways
they wanted you to perform.

When you did what they wanted,
they said "(Your name) good boy/girl";
when you didn't do what they wanted,
they said "(Your name) bad boy/girl".

This program now has independent life in your head.

In effect, you say "(Your name) good boy/girl"
to yourself at every moment it might be justified,
because this gives you happiness;
and when robbed of this opportunity,
you grouse "(Your name) bad boy/girl".

Your happiness and self-approval should depend
on the awareness that you are doing your best
and not on the events
which are only partially under your control.
Therefore you should stop rating yourself
and get the job done.


Know that rating oneself is irrelevant
because all ratings are ascribed;
they have no independent, objective reality.


Nothing is either good or bad;
goodness or badness is ascribed by an observer.


All that exists simply is.


Goodness or badness
is a function of the observer,
and exists only in the observer as observer.


Know that all self-rating
is implicit identification with the current window\*
through which you are looking;
i.e., with your current robot.


\* See page 203

Individuals often feel
that they must place themselves
on a different level from all other individuals,
either a higher or a lower level;
this is to reinforce their feelings
of being special and unique.


Therefore in rating oneself,
one is identifying with the current vehicle
and not with the universe.


Know that once you are embarked on this path,
you will begin to set up your own ambushes.

Regard these ambushes with patience and good humor,
and you will identify and conquer them;
seeking to club them out of your way
is merely another ambush.


                                  One example of an ambush:

        you may begin to implicitly ask yourself constantly
                            "Am I doing it right now"?
                         How about now? And now?" or
"Am I happy now? How about now? And now?"

                          This type of ambush guarantees misery
       by means of overzealous coveting of its opposite.

                            It leads to periods of euphoria,
when one supposes that one is doing everything right,

                                followed by sudden depression
                            when the streak seems to break.

Remember not to keep score,
simply meet each new moment as best you can
regardless of what has just transpired.


Do not try to remember all suggestions;
just remember what seems applicable
in any given moment.


Do not constantly rate your success;
answer the voices in your head
who ask how well you are doing at the moment
by saying:

"I am doing as I am doing.
You may judge it good or bad as you desire;
it is not my judgment."


*Be secure in the knowledge that you are doing your best,
and that there is nothing else to do.*


Do not feel that you can judge
your own rate of progress.

Every individual begins its evolution
against different obstacles,
and proceeds at the appropriate rate.
This rate cannot be speeded up by trying harder
or slowed down by trying too little.

All that you can do is be:
the rate of progress is a variable you cannot control
and so can essentially ignore.

Reconquer every day everything you ever conquered.
Do not expect
that the negative programs you have slayed
will stay slayed;
they will come back from different directions.

Thus your evolution is a permanent condition;
do not expect to reach an end to becoming.


Do not expect to maintain a condition of "zero defects"
even for short periods.

Your current robot is a very complex creature;
each instant there is too much going on
to guarantee sufficient attention to each stream.


Therefore, seek to allocate this scarce resource
to where it is needed at the moment,
and accept the necessity
that statistically, some things will get by you:

out of the hundreds of thousands of actions
you take in any given day,
some will be mistakes.

Expecting a 100% accuracy rate is unrealistic,
and therefore inappropriate.


Do not be impatient with yourself.

Progress seems slow because you seem to be able
to set yourself goals to act in certain ways,
and then you find that you are still acting
in other ways.

**This is because you do not have full control
of your current robot.**


If you assume that you should be able
to have complete control
of your current robot,
it is only because you are still identifying
yourself
With that robot.


You are, at any given time,
that part of you which you control.

*Youness implies control.*

You *are the one who sets goals.*

Your *robot is the one who succeeds or fails.*


If you maintain this distinction,
you will not feel negative emotion
when your robot fails,
and you will not feel inappropriate pride
when it succeeds.


Later on this path
your youness
and your control
will expand to include more of your robot
and more of the rest of the universe.

# 5.
# WHAT DO YOU WANT?:

*Stripping Away
Imposed Limitations
To Find out what
"The Me That Was Born" Wants*

Know that you are motivated too strongly
by programming
which has been impressed upon you
without your own volition.

The only way you can discover what
*you*
really want

is to scrutinize
each want you currently believe you have,

to determine why you want what you want,
and why you want or don't *want to want*
what you want.

Only in this way

can you distinguish

yourself

from the internalized others in your head.

## An Exercise:

### List the Things that You Want out of Life
### On a Sheet of Paper

*If you do this before turning the next page,
this chapter will be of far greater value to you.*

You may want
money, specific possessions,
status, fame, glory, power,
accomplishment, respect,
a large family, many lovers,
to be loved, to be known,
to be happy, health, long life,
adventure, travel,
certain feelings,
certain experiences,
etc., etc., etc.

Take a moment to think about it seriously,
and write down the list of wants
you have really been working for,
hoping for,
or not even daring
to hope for.

Put priority numbers next to your wants.
Then seek to understand,
in terms of your experiences,
why you have set
certain priorities.

After you've listed the things that you want out of life on a sheet of paper, you might want to transfer these, in priority order onto another sheet, set up something like this:

| A. List of My Wants | | | | |
|---|---|---|---|---|
| B. Who is probably most responsible for my having this want? | | | | |
| C. How much Happiness/ Unhappiness have I gotten out of having this want, so far? | | | | |
| D. Does the Real Me that existed at birth want this? | | | | |

Now, for each item on your list,
you might ask yourself the following questions:

|  |  |
|---|---|
| B. When did I first develop this want? As a result of what experience did I develop this want? Who have I known in my life who would want me to have this want? Do I have this want just to please them? |  |
| C. What is the result of my having this want? What kinds of things do I do to satisfy this want? Do these things tend to make me happy or unhappy? How good do I feel each time I satisfy this want? How bad do I feel every time I fail to satisfy this want? How much satisfaction of this want can I realistically expect out of life? Will that amount be worth the trouble? |  |
| D. Do I want this? Or am I just being the slave of my influencers by wanting this? If I had my life to start over again, would I want to have those experiences and to develop this want or would I prefer to not have those experiences and to not develop this want? Do I want to be the kind of person who has this want? |  |

For each item on your list of wants,
remember the experiences you have had
which may have led
to the development of this want.

Now visualize yourself *not* having had
those experiences,
or having had those experiences
knowing what you know now
about the unconscious influence of experience.

        Picture yourself not developing the want:

        What kind of person would you be?

        How would you be different?

        What would your face look like right now?

        How would you have acted differently so far today?

        All day yesterday?

For each want,
ask yourself is the thing you want an end in itself,
or do you just want it as a means
to satisfying another want?

For example,
if you find that you want approval by others,
is this something you want for itself,
or, do you want approval by others
as support for approving yourself?

You may find that this exercise results in a redefinition
of many of your wants,
and a simplification of the list to fewer items
which include all those on the first list.

It is conceivable that if you worked at this exercise
for a long time,
you might reduce all of the wants on your list to one;
this is a useful goal.

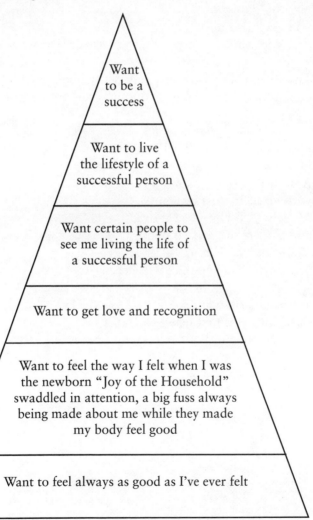

Examine your wants
to see if any of them conflict with any others.

Also, this is a good time to ask yourself
if you now want to add any wants to the list:

for example, you may now find
that you want to be the kind of person
who can free itself from wants;

you may also find
that you want to know what you really want.

These are wants that you may really have,
or you may have slavishly adopted due to our influence.


It is proper to examine these
in the same way as any other wants.
And, it is proper to compare these wants
with your first list of wants
to see which you want more,
and if there are any conflicts.

The most likely conflict will be:

which do you want more,
the things you first listed as wants,
or, to be the kind of person who knows
what he or she really wants
and can control what he or she wants?

Take the lowest priority want on the list
and tell yourself that you will no longer want it.

Explain to yourself in detail
how you will act in the future
as a result of no longer wanting it.

Listen carefully to every voice of protest which arises
against the resolution to drop this want:

list the objections,
no matter how trivial-sounding.
You may find such objections as:
"But such-and-such a person whom I admire
has such a want;
it is an admirable want."

You must then ask yourself whether the admired person
is admired because of its having that want;
or is the want irrelevant
to the reason you admire this person?

If the latter,
then the admirability of this person is not a reason
for you to have this want.


You may find, however, that there are reasons
which seem to you to be good reasons
why you should retain this want;
for example: "But I really believe
that everyone would be happier
if everyone had this want."


Proceed upward in terms of priorities
and perform this exercise with each item on the list.

Know that it is difficult
to distinguish between the voices you
hear in your head
which express what *you* really want,
and other voices
which are simply recordings
of other people's suggestions.


Thus, when you hear in your head the words:
"But I really want that!",
you must identify who that "I" is.


When you get to this stage
of arguing with yourself about what
you
really want,

you have simultaneously:

- (a) moved to a higher level of consciousness than the bulk of your species;

- (b) gotten to the hard part.


Consider dealing with the following wants, if they arise, in the following ways:

**Bodily wants:**

food, sex, sleep, warmth, rest, comfort,
pleasant sensation.

It is not you that wants these things;
it is your body.

You are not your body:
**your body is a vehicle in which you currently reside.**

Responding to your body's wants
as if they were your own
tends to identify you with your body,
causing the real you
to languish inside in ignored silence.

Whenever you become aware of a bodily want,
tell the body that it is the wanter and not you;
and then decide whether or not the real you
wants to give the body what it wants at that moment.

You may decide not to give the body what it wants
because it would distract from what the real you
is interested in doing at that moment,

or because in the long run
giving the body what it wants
will lead to the real you
being displeased
at the waste of time or at excessive weight gain, etc.


**Non-bodily wants:**

Whenever a non-bodily want arises,
test it by asking
"Might I want this so as to gain approval from others?"

If an honest, objective examination
indicates that this might be the case,
the key question must then be asked:

"What do I really gain from approval by others?"

The true answer to this question
is that one seeks approval from others
so that one feels justified in approving oneself.

The flaw in this answer
is that others may approve you
for reasons which the real you
may consider inappropriate;
for example, someone approves of you
for being strong in a situation
in which you know yourself to be
over-reacting out of weakness,
and merely pretending to be strong.

Being approved of by others
can only lead to valid self-approval
when the others in the situation
have the same knowledge and attitudes
as the individual;
and this will almost never be the case
once the individual begins to think
in the ways suggested here.

Thus, approval by others still deluded
will not lead to self-approval
by one who is no longer deluded.

Ultimately, the wanting of approval by others
can only logically lead to giving up one's freedom
to the will of these others;
and the wanting of free will
can only logically lead
to the renunciation of the desire for approval by others.

**Wanting to be approved of by others:**

this want leads to a constellation of subsidiary wants
such as wanting to be attractive, powerful, successful,
wise, self-controlled, etc.

It also leads to having approved-of attitudes
such as love of country,
contempt for certain groups,
belief in specific religious and economic systems,
interest in specific games and pastimes, etc.

The burden of all these wants and attitudes
is often borne as a means to the end
of gaining approval by others,
and not because the real you
really cares about these subsidiary wants and attitudes.

However, from long association, it is common
for the individual to believe that it really cares
about all of these subsidiary wants and attitudes.

It is precisely as if one has been told
what one must believe,
and how one must act,
in order to be approved of.

One then becomes a slave to such orders
to the extreme degree of convincing oneself
that these are one's own orders to oneself.

**Wanting of self-approval:**

this want arises out of the original goal
of maximizing positive emotion,
with which you were born.

In early life, you were shown and told by others
that certain forms of behavior on your part were good;
at those times you felt positive emotion.

Now you carry around these others and their opinions
inside yourself;

you reproduce the feelings of positive emotion
whenever you reproduce the behavior
you were told is good.

The desire for maximum positive emotion
and the desire for self-approval
are not necessarily inappropriate;
however, there are inappropriate ways
of satisfying these desires.

It is inappropriate to achieve self-approval
by achieving approval from others,
since others will usually approve you
for inferior reasons.

It is also inappropriate for you to approve yourself
for reproducing behavior you were once told is good,
since this is really the same as approving oneself
for receipt of approval by others.

To guard against this, whenever you approve yourself
you should ask
"Am I approving myself merely for behaving
in a way I once was told is good?"
If the answer is yes, the self-approval is inappropriate.

Finally, it is also inappropriate to approve yourself
for succeeding in reaching some goal
you have set for yourself
since this would logically require
that you disapprove yourself
for failing to reach such goals.

The reaching of goals
is not something that you can guarantee;
it depends not only on your effort,
but on favorable conditions you do not control,
such as the strength of your inborn
goals and equipment,
and the outside environment.

Approving or disapproving yourself
for results you only partially control
is inappropriate.


Therefore, you are left with only one basis
for approving yourself:

you may validly approve yourself
if you are doing your best
to set the proper goals and to attain them.

You may thus approve yourself regardless
of success or failure,
and regardless of the speed
at which you are progressing,
and in fact regardless
of the absence or presence of evidence of progress.

Once you are doing your best,

you are doing all you can,

thus you are to be approved.

In those cases in which you are happy
with your progress,
in which you succeed in reaching goals,
the proper response is not greater self-approval,
for this would be giving you credit for something
which the Universe has brought about with your aid,
not something which you have brought about yourself.

In such cases, the proper response is thankfulness,
happiness,
approval for the universe,
and just the same amount of self-approval
you would have given yourself
had you done your best but failed.


You may find
that you take actions of which you approve
for reasons of which you do not approve.

For example, you may find that you take actions
which add to the net value of the universe
in order to be able to feel that you are living perfectly
and are therefore justified in basking in self-love.

Attempt to maintain such useful behavior
while changing the motivation for such behavior
to more appropriate motivation;

for example,
live perfectly in order to see what ensues,
rather than to justify self-approbation.

Thus the *highest use* becomes the motivation;
the *now* becomes an end in itself;
and *results* become irrelevant.

**Wanting to be happy:**

this is a goal you were born with,
i.e., to maximize positive
and to minimize negative emotion.
It is entirely appropriate.

However, there are inappropriate ways
of achieving this goal:
for example, if you achieve happiness
as a result of achieving approval by others,
you are falling short of a much more intense happiness
it is in your power to know,
and you are tying your happiness
to an external condition
over which you do not have complete control:
thus it is a happiness which can be taken away
at the whim of others.

Achieving happiness through
satisfaction of bodily wants
is also inappropriate,
since it builds dependence
on something not fully controlled;
the necessary corollary
of happiness dependent upon the body
is misery
should the body fall ill, or into harsh surroundings;
furthermore, bodily happiness is less intense
than the happiness it is in your power to know.
This is not to say that you should avoid
bodily happiness,
merely to say that it is an insufficient goal.

The happiness that should be sought
is happiness which is totally independent
of conditions outside the mind,
while at the same time
accepting such happiness as comes from outside sources
such as the body.

It is potentially within the power of your mind
to be eternally and intensely happy regardless
of what befalls the body.

**This power of happiness is to be cultivated.**
**In part, it depends on approval**
**of the means to happiness.**
**One must first approve of one's goals,**
**and one must know that one is doing one's best**
**to achieve these goals,**
**thus achieving appropriate self-approval,**
**before the most permanent and intense happiness**
**is achievable.**

Consider adopting one or more of the following goals:

> *To be happy regardless of what happens.*
> *To add to the net value of the universe.*
>
> *To realize and fully develop*
> *one's highest possibilities.*
>
> *To discover all that may be discovered*
> *about the universe and its reasons.*
>
> *To strive for the **highest goals***
> *out of the recognition*
> *that they are the highest goals,*
> *and not out of desire for self approval.*

Once you have set *your* ultimate goals,
remind yourself of them
whenever you face any decision,
no matter how big or small,
and make *all* decisions in light of these goals.

Otherwise you may find
that you continue to make decisions
so as to preserve former ways of acting
and not the new ways.

It is a common foible to lose sight
of ultimate goals,
and to instead concentrate on interim goals
in ways inimical
to the ultimate goals;

*avoid this trap.*


In setting and pursuing your own goals,
you are freeing yourself from the will of others,
even insofar as their will has become imbedded in you
and has disguised itself as you.

Therefore also reject the values placed on things
by others.

All value is ascribed;
there is no value in any thing
except insofar as someone ascribes such value.
Hesitate therefore to yourself
before ascribing value to any thing;

everything in the universe
has equal right to be there.
(Everything in the universe
also has equal responsibility
to improve itself.)

Listen respectfully therefore to every communication,
whether from inside or outside of you,
and evaluate its cause;
strive to understand its cause; respond accordingly.

Take seriously, for example,
each message from your mind, even if it displeases you;
a harsh rejection
will not remove a displeasing message from your mind,
but will merely drive it underground
from where it will be able to work against you
in secrecy.

Be gentle with all who communicate with you,
including your own mind.


Many strive to follow the rules set down by others
more than they strive to listen to their own messages;
many take more seriously
the tasks given to them by others
than they take the tasks implicit in their own thoughts.

Give each part of the universe
the respect you give the whole;

do not devalue small voices inside
simply because they seem unbecoming;
they may seem unbecoming
only because others have told you
that certain ways of feeling are unbecoming.


Listen with respect, and then make your own decisions.

# 6.

## OPENING THE SENSES:

### *Seeing more of what Is*

Observe yourself observing the scene.

Imagine what you look like;

imagine that a mirror which only you can see
exists on the far wall.

Do not get so involved in your task or role
that you cannot see yourself in this mirror.

Catch your facial expressions and hand gestures,
body movements and so forth in this mirror,
and ask yourself
why you have created these manifestations.

Unstitch yourself from the moment

by looking down at the whole scene

from the ceiling.

Question your own possible biases
which may affect what you see.

Strip away your own interpretations
to get back to the things themselves.


If you see "ugliness" or feel "pain",
separate the "ugliness" or "pain"
(which are interpretations or conclusions,
not observations)
from what is really there;
an unnamed, unlabelled vision or feeling.


                    Remember that you must look longer
                                    to see beauty
                              than to see ugliness,
              since ugliness resides in the associations
                which others have communicated to you,
                          while beauty resides
                          in the next closer layer to reality.


Remember that words have a physical impact on you,
so that you must guard against
becoming influenced by them.

Remember that you are influenced telepathically
by moods of others,
so that you must guard against
being influenced by these.

Remember that your senses
are altered by what they perceive,
so that you will perceive things differently
based upon what you have perceived before;

*strive to strip away such sensory channeling
by looking at everything
as if seeing it for the first time*


*without allowing yourself to label
what you see
with words in your head.*


Toy with alternate explanations for events.


Allow your imagination free reign
to propose the most unbelievable such explanations

which seem, however, to be the simplest
and most direct ways
of describing what happens.


For example, if entities in a situation
seem to get carried away
as a result of the blandishments of one entity,

allow this to appear to you as the latter entity
magically hooking the others into a game.


For example, if you note that each entity
appears to influence others
even before he begins to speak,

allow this to appear to you
as a force-field-like phenomenon.

For example, if you note
that your hands seem to know
how to massage another entity,

allow yourself to see this
as your hands being programmed
by the other entity's body consciousness.


For example, if you seem to be acting
as if you were under the sway
of a hindering telepathic force,

allow yourself to verbalize this
in an "as if" mode.


For example, if you seem to be acting
as if you had a stupidity program in your head,

allow yourself to verbalize this
in an "as if" mode.


Root assumptions about reality
are imbedded in the very syntax of our language.

These root assumptions tend to restrict the ways
in which we are able to look at things.

It is useful to minimize all such restrictions.

One way of doing this
is to toy with "as if"
or "magical" explanations for events;

these sometimes allow verbalizations
of simple organizing principles
which otherwise would not be verbalized
due to "scientific or materialistic" biases
in our language itself.


Do not screen out or rephrase statements to yourself
which utilize models
other than the scientific/materialistic:

e.g., magic,
physical reality is illusion,
telepathy, reincarnational selves,
solipsism, other consciousness in your head,
God, you as one manifestation of God, etc.

Allow yourself to express yourself in any way
that seems to most simply and directly fit the facts.

Treat such statements
as trial balloons
from part of your consciousness
and do not identify with the statements
or attach yourself to them via belief.


Consider all such models
(including the scientific/materialistic)
to be theoretically possible ways
of describing
objective reality,

*and resist the temptation*
*to place any such model*
*above any other*

except very tentatively,
unless and until a point is reached
at which no doubt is conceivable
based on the evidence you yourself experience
without the possibility of hallucination.

This suspension of belief regarding worldview
should in no way restrain your free use
of whichever of these models
seems most direct and useful at the moment.


Treat your every experience
as a communication from somewhere,

and therefore ask:


*Why did that happen?*

*What is it trying to tell me?*


Therefore, when you observe something,
observe that you observed it,

and ask:


*Why did I notice that?*


Allow yourself to verbalize to yourself
any connections you intuit
between a current situation
and a memory.

If you do not yet see in what way
the two are connected,
merely state to yourself:

I appear to perceive some sort of connection
between X and Y.


Explore the perceived connection
but do not attempt to force yourself
to understand why you perceive the connection,
for such forcing
may cause you to persuade yourself
of a false connection.


*Keep the apparent connection in mind,
and eventually your reasons for the connection
will also become apparent.*


Make the most
general
observations

rather than the most detailed.

Remember that the pervasive tends to become invisible.


Therefore see the most pervasive elements
of any situation.
Look at the field or background.

Fuse the separate instances into an overall principle.

State to yourself that which is so
obvious
about a situation,
that none could disagree with it.

Do not screen out observations
that are so obvious as to seem trivial;
you will automatically tend to verbalize
only those observations which are,
or which will become relevant.

Do not attempt to force any such observations
to have immediate relevance;

you may only much later discover
your reasons
for making an observation.

*Count the feel*
*of a situation*
*more important than the look.*

Each time you find yourself
in the company of other entities,
ask yourself:

- How would a total stranger, entering this scene at this moment, perceive the role each entity is playing?

- If I look at this situation as a child might, what do I see?

- Assuming the existence of (conscious or unconscious) telepathic activity at all times, what is each entity trying to do here telepathically?

- What is motivating each entity in this situation?

These questions strip away the specific words
and physical details of a situation
to reveal the underlying reality of

"What's going on here?"

They de-emphasize detail
in order to focus your inner senses,
intuition and telepathic abilities*
on the essence behind the illusions.

---

\* We do not assert these. Let us simply not rule them out.

In effect, these questions describe a perspective
it is possible for you to adopt
which focuses not so much on

*what*
is happening

as on

*why*
it is happening.


Ultimately
you will be able to maintain this perspective
without asking any of the above questions.

The questions are temporary devices
which both describe
and also tend to stimulate the perspective.


The universal plan moves forward
via interactions of consciousness.


At a basic level,
all that exists are these interactions,
with sense information representing
the symbol shadows of these interactions.


Therefore focus on the observation
of the consciousness interactions
which are taking place below the level
of sense information;

i.e., make your observations excluding sense information
except as documentation.

For example, go from "He spilled the liquid" to
"He is very nervous whenever in my presence —
why?"

In other words, treat all entities as immaterial

and focus on their interactions

exclusive of the material sense information

which symbolized these interactions.

> Be aware of the emotions radiated
> by each entity including yourself.

> When you detect and identify an emotion present,
> ask yourself why it is there and who is radiating it.

Remember that there are causes for every effect;

therefore note every manifestation
(word, tone of voice, facial gestures, etc.)
of each entity, including yourself,

and ask yourself what might be the causes
for such manifestations.

Monitoring your own manifestations in this way
will tend to reduce your undeliberate manifestations.

Learn to assimilate experience
by striving to see
all of the implications of each observation.

Attempt to trace causes back to their causes, and so on.

Also look into the future
and see where a situation is lkely to go
(alternate paths)
if left alone,
and where you might help it go by selective action.


In other words, ask yourself

*How might this have gotten started?*

And:

*How might I turn this to everyone's advantage?*


When confronted with observations that appear negative, ask yourself:

*What good things might these be bad manifestations of?*


You will find, if you search carefully enough,
that all situations of loss
are actually opportunities for positive change,

and that **all flaws
are actually manifestations of strengths
which have not yet found outlets.**

Look for the most general knowledge inherent
in the observation of the observation.


For example, go from "He is mad at me" to
"This issue always seems to cause a strain between us";

from "I see an interesting new viewpoint on this subject"
to "How can I apply this interesting new viewpoint
to other subjects?";

from "Now I know how to do X"
to "Why is it that I always want to find out
how to do things such as X?"


This is a process of analyzing
each observation
from every standpoint
one can generate within time,
energy and interest constraints.

In this process, the specific detail observation
is fitted into the larger information systems
of your mind,

so that you spend as little time as possible
regarding the specific detail observation in itself,

*and as much time as possible regarding
the larger information systems themselves
in light of the new specific detail observations.*

# 7.

# STAYING FOCUSED THROUGH COMPLEXITY:

## *Effectively Dealing With Many Things at Once*

*Array your attention so as to keep track of —
i.e., remember —*

each relevant jobstream coming in at the moment.


For example,
imagine that you are piloting a vehicle
in a traffic-stream
with other vehicles/survival-danger.

You must direct your attention to this task,
which let us assume,
breaks up into two relevant jobstreams:

looking out ahead,

and looking behind
via a rear-view mirror.


Simultaneously these other relevant
jobstreams are going on:

Other entities in the vehicle with you
are communicating to you.


Let us say that there are four entities,
each communicating to you
on separate (although possibly related) subject;

Each of these four entities
is not only communicating to you verbally,
but is also saying things to you via tone of voice, etc.,
and is also potentially transmitting information to you
on a telepathic level
(although not necessarily consciously).

Let us say that these entities represent
four more jobstreams
which you want to keep track of:

you want to understand
what these entities are really saying,
what is really motivating them to say these things, etc.


Useful words are coming into your head from somewhere
(subconscious, the Universe, your own Higher Self, etc. —
these labels may all be labelling the same thing).

You want to keep track of these words,
i.e. remember them so that you can write them down later.


This is another jobstream.

We have chosen such a difficult state
in which to keep track of — i.e., remember —
the minutes of each jobstream,
so as to outline a method which is applicable
to all states
including such difficult ones.


It may be easier to appreciate
the usefulness of the method
in relation to such extreme cases,

although every moment of existence
also involves a considerable clamor for attention,
not much less difficult
than the one in our example.


The difficulty of dealing with "normal clamor"
is demonstrated by numerous examples,
of which we will specify one:


Most entities wearing a timepiece or watch

forget

what time it is

as soon as they look up

from their watch.

Consciousness in its "normal" state
is not capable of focusing attention
on multiple jobstreams,
and needs a specific method of doing so.
Here, back in our seven-stream example,
is such a method:

                                              Monitor all streams.

            Rotate attention so that in the space of a short time,
                            all seven streams are scanned.

                This is like looking into the rear-view mirror
                                  from time to time,
                      but with more mirrors to check;

                          each entity is a "mirror",

            your own head-stream is a "mirror", etc.


Do not add to any stream
and do not get caught up in any stream:

simply look at each stream long enough
for what is happening there
to come into sharp focus.


*Avoid using words in your head to analyze the stream.*
*Do not get attached to the possible results*
*of any stream.*
*Simply look at what is there.*

Keep looking until a feeling of conviction
arises of itself
that you understand the stream —
or until it is time to shift to another stream
(understanding may come on the next sweep,
or a later one).

Treat the words-in-your-head-stream as a monolog
being directed to you from outside:
in other words,
as another conversation
you have to keep track of.

Unless you do this,
it is highly likely
that you will turn back to your head-stream
and find that you cannot remember
what you were thinking of
just a few moments ago.

But if you treat the head-stream as another entity
talking to you,
you are much more likely
to keep track of
the jist of his or her remarks.


The second aspect of the method
(looking at what is there until it focuses itself)
needs more explication.

The total consciousness needs time to calculate.
This time need varies based on what is to be calculated.

For example, looking at the traffic-stream
takes only an instant
to calculate how to react to it;

but looking at a work of art
may take considerably longer to calculate
the full telepathic response
to what is being communicated.


Use of words in the head generally slows down
this calculation process.

Merely looking,
remaining empty of words,
is the fastest means of calculating.


This can be demonstrated as follows:

Look at a work of art not seen before.
Keep words away.
Note how gradually you begin to see things
you did not see at first;
how they begin to form a pattern;
how you begin to get possible glimmerings
of what the artist intended,
of where he or she was at.


What you are sensing
is the consciousness in the solution process;
over time,
sharper and sharper focus solutions are appearing.

Most entities, unaware of this process,
react prematurely
by selecting an early soft-focus solution
and stopping the process;
or by rejecting the early soft-focus solution
and saying "I don't get it",
and turning away.


Words in the head interfere with the solution process
except when they are used sparingly
to clarify amorphous blobs.


Words like "Let's see now ..." and
"What could that mean?", etc.
are of the counter-productive kind:

they are signs of trying to manipulate
using only the intellect portion
of the consciousness.


Words like "Give and Take"
or "Equilibrium", etc.
tend to be of the productive kind,
in that such words
will pop into your head
as models of what is going on
and will result in a clearer understanding
of what you already
were beginning to grasp
fuzzily.

Learn to distinguish between
the brushstroke-model words
which your total consciousness yields
in and of itself,

and the obsessive-manipulative words
which you consciously program
and which add nothing
but take up time.

> *Look without talking to yourself about it
> but accept useful words which float up
> unbidden.*

The solution process
is the reason why the longer you avoid closure,
the better the solution you get.

**Avoid the tendency to take out a half-baked cake.**

When it is ready,
you will know;
conviction will be great.

Then wait a bit longer and test the conviction.

Conviction per se is not a sure sign.
Conviction which withstands
a devil's advocate approach
is a reasonably sure sign.

Give yourself time
to mount a suitably strong
devil's advocate test.
Do not hurry understanding
lest you get mis-understanding
as a quick-and-dirty
solution.

# 8.

## "In Action, Watch the Timing"

*— Tao Te Ching
of Lao Tsu*

Act only when you decide
that the loss in value associated with delay
is probably greater
than the gain in value associated with thinking further
about the motives, possible consequences,
and alternatives to such action.


Start now.
Do not move any part of your body
from the position it is now in.
Regard any such movement
as an action to be evaluated prior to action.

If you have a feeling that you want to change position,
search inside you for the source of that feeling:

>is it that the body wants to move
>into a position more comfortable to it?
>
>Is it that you want to go get something?
>What part of you wants that something, and why?
>
>Do you feel you should respond to someone
>who is looking at or talking to you now?
>Why do you feel you should respond?
>
>Are you curious
>about something that is now going on nearby?
>Why are you curious?
>
>What specifically will you gain by looking?
>Why do you want to gain this?

*If you question yourself
as deeply as you can learn how to,
prior to even what seems to be
the most trivial of actions,
you will suddenly discover*

*a whole new state of reality.*


Progress through a personal appraisal at natural speed
prior to action.
Be aware of, but unmindful of, voices and feelings
which tell you that you must decide now
or must take action now.

                                      These voices and feelings
are a force that has had power over you until now;
they originate in society;
society which expects you to perform in certain ways.
Society has conditioned you to perform,
not to appraise.


Give precedence to your own judgment:

critically evaluate all information,
whether it comes to you from inside or from the outside,

and then make your own decision
based on that evaluation.

Do not move

but observe yourself not complete the intended act.


You have not changed position;

you have not gotten up to get something;
you have not responded to your friend
and you have not looked at what is going on nearby.


You can visualize in detail
what it would have been like
to have done any of these things;
you can see how others would have reacted.


Having done none of these things,
you can see that the world has not come to an end,

although your body may be uncomfortable
and your friends may wonder why
you are strangely immobile.

*By having called a moratorium on undeliberated action,
you have entered a deeper level of thought.*


The greater and the more continuous the periods
over which you let such a moratorium prevail,
the deeper will be the level of thought you attain.


And there are depths currently unimaginable to you.

Your objective in communicating with others
is to find out what information they are working with
that you may not be working with,
so that you can evaluate it for yourself.


Your objective in communication
is not to establish for others the greater rightness
of your viewpoints;

such greater rightness applies only for yourself:
each other individual
should set its own decision above yours.


Thus, if your friends believe that you are strange
because you are immobile while you deliberate action,

but you are testing whether this is a useful means
of thinking more deeply,

then you should remove all force
from the feelings inside you
which tell you to move
in ways which will reassure your friends.

Live each scene as if nothing else exists
in the past,
present or future.
Do not let yourself think beyond the current scene
to the next one;
this is evidence that you are doing the current scene
to get past it,
rather than doing it for its own sake.


Avoid activities that you would do
merely to have them done;
i.e., activities which are satisfying
only in their elimination.
Get the maximum out of the current activity:
immerse yourself in the moment.


        Make each movement a deliberate one;
        hurrying is usually evidence that you are trying
        to get the activity over with,
        rather than getting the most out of the activity.

        Hurrying is rarely justified
        and almost always deleterious.

If you detect that you are impatient
to reach a decision
on a subject you are thinking about,
temporarily put the subject aside
and think first
about the subject of why you are in a hurry.


Do you want to get through thinking
so that you can engage in another specific activity?

If so, then think about which activity
you really want to engage in now.


If you are going to put off thinking
until a time when you really want to do it
and can therefore do it with total immersion,

then write down
whatever you have already established about that subject
in your thinking
which might be forgotten.


Writing your thoughts down
should have the effect
of freeing your mind from the subject completely,

so that you can go on
to fully immerse yourself

in whatever other activity
you would rather be doing now.

**Slow down thinking
until you can see each thought.**

This is the most direct payoff of non-rushing:

when thought itself progresses at natural speed,
the speed at which the thinker is aware
of the full meaning of each word
and fleeting image,

the probability of right decisions
vastly increases.

Judge slowly but make progress with every statement.

Do not seek to resolve matters,
but rather seek to add to the solution process.

**The longer you restrain yourself from a final solution,
while adding relevant and maximally objective observations,
the higher you raise the probability of right decisions.**

The quicker you reach positive or negative judgment
the more you are leaving out:

you are not seeing the positive opportunities
hiding in something you reject,

or you are not seeing the pitfalls to be overcome
in something you accept.

Consider *all* of the ways
you observe yourself use time as *projects*,
and review them in light of allocation
within available time;

specific friends, vocations, avocations,
periods of seeming rest, and so on:


all of these reflect implicit goals
which you have to make explicit
and weigh in relation to the others.


In all of these activities
you are engaging in self-selected work
to express yourself and actualize your goals;

therefore find out what it is specifically
that you want to get
out of each of these activities,


and allocate each activity
the appropriate proportion of your time
so that each can make progress
at its own natural speed.

Keep all projects moving forward.

If you find that you have a number of projects,
allocate your time among these
in a way which will maximize achievement
of your goals.


This allocation may result
in some low-priority projects
being shelved temporarily or permanently,
passed on to others or combined into other projects.

Constantly adjust your list of projects
and time allocations to projects

so as to keep all projects moving forward
at natural speed.


**In all things, move forward at natural speed.**


Avoid the common tendency to go faster;
this usually results in greater speed
but less intensity of development.

The intensity with which you can experience
and realize your own creativity
is more important
than meeting self-imposed deadlines.

Inspection of self-imposed deadlines
usually reveals them
to be internalized-other-people's deadlines.

*The time you spend not creating
may also be essential to the fullest development
of your creativity.*

Strive to achieve an appropriate balance
between time spent *doing*
versus time spent *not doing*.

If you spend too much time doing,
your conscious mind will block the functioning
of your subconscious mind,
and you will interfere
with the stream of consciousness
coming from the latter to the former.

If you spend too much time not doing,
you will underactualize your own goals.

If you always do what you want to do
at any given moment,

this will help you to automatically achieve
an appropriate balance between doing
and not doing, for there will be times
when you will not want to do anything:

at such times,
do not try to work at anything,

but simply flow with what is happening

into directions you find yourself naturally seeking.


Set achievable time goals

based on objective review
of your own past performance.
Emotionlessly revise these goals
if they are revealed to be too ambitious.


There is a tendency to understate
the time requirements for any task,
based on such factors
as not seeing all of the steps
which will be required until the task is underway,

or not seeing all of the distractions
which will inevitably occur
and must be allowed for.

> Compensate for this tendency
> by undershooting when setting time goals
> (it is *not* necessary to undershoot
> with respect to *what* you hope to achieve).

On occasion, you will note
that you sit down to do a task
at a moment when you have just received useful input
to that task from another quarter:

obviously, it would have been unfortunate
had you forced yourself to begin that task sooner,
without the benefit of the input which just arrived.

This is a specific instance
of the benefits to be gained by non-rushing

and by accepting what happens as relevant
even if it does not seem so.


Assertion of your will
as dominant over the will of input

requires that you place yourself, at any given moment,
in the precise number of input streams
you are willing to accept at that moment.


If you desire to have no input other than your own,
you must be alone and inaccessible
to communication of any kind;

this is an extremely valuable state
that is too rarely used:
many individuals are alone only when they are comatose.

By submission to any and all input streams,
most individuals have forgotten themselves,
and are slavishly programmed by their inputs.

You, however, know that you have a mission;
and this mission can only be interpreted and executed
by looking inside.

*Remember who you are, remain awake,*
*focus on your own goals:*
*control the valve which lets in distractive inputs.*

This may contrast sharply with the more common state
of diffusing the consciousness
across many streams of uncontrolled input
which are allowed to demand of you
at their convenience,
with you in a constant state of adaptation,
slavishly trying to cope
with all of these streams at once.

In this common state,
you engage several inputs at once,
without full motivation or preparation,

and are vaguely conscious of a sense of disquiet
at being trapped in such activities
without full desire and preparation;

simultaneously,
other inputs are piling in,
in front of and behind these current ones.

The usual product of this common state is confusion,
indecision, and self-loathing.
This state is brought about
by submission to the will of the input;
i.e., you agree that any input
has the right to communicate itself to you
at its will, not yours.


Program yourself for action before engaging in it.

Review your goals for the upcoming activity.

Have a waking dream
in which you see yourself engaging in the activity;
this will alert you to contingencies
so as to arm you
with contingency plans.

Program the environment
by eliminating possibilities of distraction,
and by having the right tools for the job handy.

Do not be lazy about getting the right tools first;
this will turn out to be false economy of time.

*If you try to do something too soon*
*It will snag.*


*You saw it,*
*Now let it happen in the dance.*

# 9.

# DIS-IDENTIFYING WITH THE THOUGHT SENATE

*Not Throwing your Authority
Behind Untested Head Spewings*

Visualize the mechanism
which sends you verbal thought messages
not as one speaker,

*but as a vast senate of many different speakers.*

Each experience you have had
creates a separate viewpoint
from which comments may be made.

Therefore, the first step to take
in analyzing any thought sent to you,

*is to determine who is speaking:*

which set of experiences that you have had
is expressing its viewpoint to you?

**Do not identify with your thoughts.
You are not the thinker of the thoughts;**

**you are the hearer of the thoughts.**


The thinker of your thoughts
is a subsidiary mechanism within you,
which attempts to put some of your feelings
into words;

you must then assess the way you feel
about these words.


Not looking at the matter this way,
most individuals tend to identify themselves
as the author of the words in their head,
and consequently are biased in favor
of believing and defending these thoughts.


In fact, each thought you have
is merely a *trial balloon,*
a draft from your speechwriter
sent to you

so that you can decide whether you agree or disagree.

In many cases, you will realize
that the speaker of the last thought sent to you

is representing the viewpoint
of some other individual(s) you have known,
often in the exact words and tone of voice
used by these other individuals.


Obviously, accepting such viewpoints as your own
would be submitting to mental slavery.
Yet this is precisely what most individuals do,

by identifying with their thoughts.


After you have identified the last speaker,
engage him or her in a dialog
in which you ask the speaker to defend his or her position
by asking the speaker specific questions
which illuminate possible flaws in his or her position.


*In this way,*
*you will always be questioning your own last thought*
*in a search for objective truth,*

separated from the conditioning effects
of your experience
and from the influence
of communications you have received.

As you question your own last thought,
search the senate of your experiences
for other speakers
who can give evidence one way or the other.
Attempt to prove or disprove
the original speaker's position
based on empirical evidence and not on hearsay.


Be especially wary of certain speakers
who have gained great clout in your senate.

They will interrupt a dialog
with great force and persuasion
and seem to immediately set a given matter to rest;
the instant conviction that you,
The Listener To The Senate,
feel is *closure* and the elimination of dissonance.


Immediately reopen the matter
by seeking to discover the identity
of this persuasive speaker.

You will know
that a given speaker is one of this type
when you hear his or her words spoken
with great emphasis or emotion,

and when you immediately find yourself
tending to agree with certainty
born of long association with the particular ideas
he or she is expressing.

Although you may have always accepted
the advice of this senator in the past,
now is the time
to subject him or her
to the same critical questioning as everyone else.


Be especially aware of certain senators
who are never given a chance to speak in your senate.

These will generally be those
who have opposed
your forceful and persuasive speakers;
often these opposing voices never reached you as words.

Whenever you resolve to do something
but do not follow through on your resolution,
it is because these unheard voices are
throwing their boots in the machinery.

Until you have an unrestricted dialog on such issues,
the "enemy within"
that you think you have vanquished
(by refusing to listen to him or her)
has arguments you haven't even heard of yet.

Thus be careful to keep track
of each little voice in your head;
don't shout anyone down;
treat each as if he or she deserves an answer.

Let a speaker express himself or herself
although he or she appears to you
to be shabby,
immoral, stupid, lazy, childish,
unattractive,
naive, venal, egotistical, awkward, weak or insane.

Develop a knack
for hearing the muffled voices in your mind.

Take each viewpoint seriously enough
to justify a dialog.

In effect,
you have been screening out certain thoughts
as being unworthy of putting before the senate;

listen closely to recapture these thoughts
the next time they are fleetingly whispered
or intimated;

you will find that there is value in debating them.


Do not push your senate to reach unanimous conclusions.


Many individuals, finding themselves to be
internally divided on a given issue,
will implicitly decide
that they do not want to be so divided,
and will set out to support
all of the arguments of one side
and demolish all of the arguments of the other side.

In so doing they will be forced to accept
certain unproven premises.

In effect, this process is the same
as choosing which way to be prejudiced.

As a result of this process,
the individual sells himself or herself
a black and white position
which he or she wants to believe
in order to simplify things.

Dissenting voices are muffled
but not expunged,
and remain around to impede action
which is justified
based on the falsified unanimous vote.


To guard against this state,
learn to accept the fact
that two opposing views may each retain some merit,
and be suspicious of all black and white notions.

Gently educate yourself away from a desire to believe
to an ability to suspend belief.
Remember that anyone who wants to believe
can be misled.

Do not seek to close issues permanently,
but merely to adopt tentative temporary positions
to be reviewed again and again.

*Keep questioning every position.*

Seek truth
but categorize everything you feel to be true

as a useful fiction,
a useful way of looking at things,
a useful way of describing things.

Discard a useful fiction
when a more useful fiction becomes available.


Be wary of the senator
who will get you to act impulsively
on seemingly trivial matters
by saying (implicitly):
"I know it's a silly thing to do
but let's do it and get it over with
rather than waste more time by thinking about it."

The flaw in this senator's position
is that in the aggregate,
the sum of all inappropriate actions
which will be allowed to occur
using this line of reasoning,
will represent the great bulk of all actions.

Even inappropriate emotions and thoughts
will be allowed to slip through
under cover of this imprimatur.

Humoring this senator can only lead to grief,

since it is *only by treating nothing as trivial*

*that you build the strength of your will*

*and hence your ability to change your mind*

*or your mood at will.*

It is only by maintaining discipline continuously
that you empower your discipline

to overcome any and all of your tendencies

to act or to feel
contrary to your will.

Maintain continuity of will
by starting the effort all over again
each instant,
regardless of what has gone before.

Do not act impulsively
if there is the slightest trace of doubt present;

give precedence to any senator who asks a question,
over any senator who demands action.

Accept the multitudinousness of questions
to be considered.

You will find that each question
gives rise to several prior questions.

In this way, you will begin
with a seemingly simple question,
hear the views of several senators on the question,
seek to identify each senator who has spoken,
and question each one's viewpoint.

It may seem to you that real progress
beyond the first seemingly simple question
is arduous and time-consuming;
and you may become overwhelmed
by the enormity of the task
of treating each of the hundreds of questions,
which have already occurred to you in this fashion.

You may see yourself as regressing infinitely backwards,
going more and more deeply into the questions
underlying your first seemingly simple question,
with no apparent hope of ever laying it to rest
and going on to all of the later questions.

This infinite regressing
is actually the path forward.

Do not be in a hurry to have considered all questions,
because you will never have considered all of them;
more will always arise to be considered.

Maintain a list of questions to be considered,
so that none will be lost;

knowing that none will be lost
and you will always have a long waiting list,

do not be concerned with getting through the list,

for this is an endless process.


The first question to consider is:

What is the first question
I want to or need to consider?


Thus,
you may find that you want to go through your list
and establish priorities,
which may reflect outside pressures
requiring action decisions.

However, the first question may be:

Why don't I want to start considering these questions?
Or: Why am I in a hurry?

Always attack the immediate problem;

if there is any negative emotion,
this represents the immediate problem.

Seek to establish the proper attitude for thinking
before beginning to think about substantive issues;
thus, always start with the questions concerning method
after negative emotion has been removed.

Finally, get on to substantive issues
in the order in which
you have decided to consider them.


When you feel you have exhausted
all of the possible thoughts
you might have about an issue,
and dissonance remains,
do not be discouraged:

this means that there is more to think about
which might not be immediately apparent.


This is an exciting opportunity
to do two things:

attack the problem creatively
from unlikely new angles;

and put the problem to your subconscious,
telling it to contact you when it has any ideas.

Reaching this "apparent dead end dissonance"
is cause for joy,
since it means that all necessary
linear exercises
have been successfully engaged in
and their residue cleared away.


Keep asking "Why?";
regress through layer after layer of prior assumptions;

peel away your beliefs, reasons, feelings and desires
until you reach a point on a given issue
where all you are left with
is intuition
as to your
seemingly innate leaning.

For example:

> Senator: *We don't seem to want to eat meat any more. I wonder why that might be?*
>
> Senator: *I've noticed that too. Perhaps it could be a revulsion against taking life.*
>
> Senator: *But we've been through that before. There is no evidence that death is final, and it seems a useful fiction to postulate a benevolent universe in the absence of contrary evidence. So why have revulsion at eating meat?*
>
> Senator: *Could we be influenced in this by our vegetarian friends?*

(At this point, you feel around inside you, trying this self-prediction on for size. Test all self-predictions in this way.)

Senator: *I don't think that's it; it doesn't feel right.*

Senator: *Are you sure? Are you sure that we aren't subconsciously trying to play the "saint" role?*

Senator: *(Having felt around inside) I don't think so; that doesn't feel right either. There are no memories of feeling virtuous at times when we have rejected meat; the meat rejections were more off-hand, mixed moods dominated mostly by other considerations.*

Senator: *Could it be sloppy-minded sentimentalism, characterized by images of cute little animals, that we are acting on illogically despite our acceptance of the useful fiction of a benevolent universe? If that's the case, shouldn't we either trash the "benevolent universe" idea or go back to eating meat, in order that we are internally consistent?*

Senator: *Why be internally consistent? Also, there have been recent occasions on which we have been unemotional at the fact of the death of various beings including animals; this is evidence that we do have conviction about the "benevolent universe" idea. At those times, we obviously would have been less unemotional if we were given to picturing images of cute little animals in the context of death.*

Senator: *(Having felt around inside) No, I don't think that the sentimentalism hypothesis rings true inside.*

(The discussion continues until the senators have ceased generating hypotheses about why you have stopped wanting to eat meat.)

Senator: *We don't seem to be giving up meat for any silly reasons we have been able to think of so far. Perhaps our Master\* simply doesn't feel like it currently.*

(The senators may or may not notice a rumbling bass vibration of conviction throughout the mind and body.)

Senator: *(Having felt around inside) Yes, that feels right. Let's go along with it until some new evidence presents itself on this issue. Next issue ...*

Senator: *Wait! Are we sure that we aren't fooling ourself? Is it really the Master who wants this, or are we pretending to know His/Her desires?*

Senator: *(Having felt around inside) I get no feeling of doubt on this issue. Let's leave it to the subconscious council and get on to issues where we have tangible doubt right now.*

(End of example.)

---

\* See next page.

The Master
may be defined
as that part of you
which existed prior
to any outside influence,

and which still exists
underneath all the layers
of outside influence
which you have absorbed.


The senate in you exists
to interpret the Master's will,
by putting words together
and testing to see
if these words feel like a valid expression
of the Master's unspoken position.

The Master itself rarely if ever speaks in language.

The Master is the source of intuition as well as will.
The Master is that aspect of you
which is the connection point
between your seemingly individual consciousness
and the universal consciousness;
that is, *your Master is also everyone else's Master.*

(This is a useful fiction or it is true.)


When your senate has stripped away all reasons
for your doing something
but your Master still wants to do it,

you act in freedom.

When your senate has stripped away
all of the justifications
for taking a certain position
but your Master still wants to take that position,

you have reached right judgment.


However, you can rarely if ever be *certain*
that it is in fact your Master
that wants you to act or think
in a certain way;

thus, you must go along with what you feel
to be the Master's will
only when there is no doubt left
in any part of the senate,
and only until any new evidence
creates any such doubt.

When there is doubt,
the senate must work the issue over until resolved
at which point it should be turned over
to the subconscious
until a later senate session.

A list may be kept of items
assigned to the subconscious.

Another list may be kept of agenda items for upcoming
senate sessions.

## *Mindquiet*

Learn to detect the types of situations
in which you should *not* interrupt
an action in progress,
despite the sudden uneasiness
which tells you that you should
stop and think about it.

These are often situations involving other people
who will in effect not give you time to think;
and if you stop and think,
you will be removing some of your attention
needed to deal effectively
with such people.


In these situations, tell yourself "Mindquiet"

and refuse to listen to any words
emanating from your mind
until you declare the Mindquiet period
to be over.

Then bring all of your attention to bear
on the external situation,
either flowing with it
or imposing your own will on it,
as dictated by your intuition,

with a tendency to flow with
unless the intuition to do otherwise
is strong and clear
and feels right.

Know that any important thoughts
you have during Mindquiet
will not be lost,
but will recur later.

If brief relevant self-commands arise during Mindquiet
(e.g. "Do your best and accept whatever happens"
or "See how you can add to the net value
of the universe", etc.)
accept their wisdom
but do not answer them or think about them;
remain fully immersed
in the current three-dimensional reality.

Put off closure entirely during Mindquiet,
resolving to come back
and think about the situation in detail afterwards,
if there is an afterwards.


Not all situations demanding Mindquiet
will involve other people;
some overwhelming states of consciousness
also demand Mindquiet.

Be prepared to shift into Mindquiet
and intuitive functioning
whenever there is imminent survival-danger,
when other people are not giving you time to think,
when in an altered-consciousness state,
or when feeling extreme negative emotion
and thinking appears to be increasing
such negative emotion
rather than removing it.

By removing an additional source of frustration,
Mindquiet will tend to have a calming effect.

# 10.

# Improving Inner Visibility:

## *Allowing a Wider Range of Material Through the Verbalizer*

Know that the main value
of developing
your powers of observation
is realized
when you turn these powers inward:

*head action
seen frame
by
frame
is revelational.*

You can learn more by turning
the spotlight inward for a minute
than you can
from all that you observe
externally in a lifetime.

This is especially true of self-observation
during behavior you regard as most trivial
or habitual.

The ultimate objective is to see

each separate move

your mind makes.


This requires focused attention
based on the speed of action
and on the fact that the head action
is at first perceived only dimly,
as a result of long outward focus.

Example:

> You are in a sensitive state. You are engaged in a task which confronts you with new input at a rate not determined by you, such as catching objects thrown by another entity and placing them on the ground.
>
> Simultaneously, you are able to sense your environment. You suddenly smell something, and before analyzing it, the other entity throws an object and you must catch it. This distracts you from analyzing the smell.
>
> You catch the object and place it on the ground, now aware of the smell as an unpleasant one. You suddenly feel something in your back, and an instant later categorize the feeling as a minor pain. You begin to worry slightly. Your face shows joylessness, and you begin to worry about what the other entity will think about this.

What has happened
is that certain head action has gone past which, in the
example as stated thus far,
is mostly invisible.

We will now show the action.


All sense data are encoded,
i.e., must be interpreted;

thus, depending upon your mood,
you can see the same object
as dull or interesting, etc.

In the same way,
a smell may be interpreted
as pleasant or unpleasant:
a strong organic smell may be interpreted
as pleasant if food is seen simultaneously,
while it may be regarded as unpleasant
if excrement is seen simultaneously.


*Distractions tend to cause negative feelings;*

a very minor distraction
may cause a very minor negative feeling.
Even such a very minor negative feeling, however,
may have enough energy to cause an olfactory datum
to be interpreted negatively.
Thus, in being distracted by the need
to catch the thrown object,
you categorize the smell as unpleasant,
simply as a result of distraction.

*The senses are altered by what they perceive;*

thus once having received a negative input
from the environment,
you are more likely
to interpret succeeding input as negative.
The feeling in your back
(another part of the environment),
which might have been sensible as a pleasant ache,
was sensed as pain.


*Discomfort tends to generalize;*

thus once having smelled a bad smell
and felt a bad feeling,
you begin to worry about
subject after subject.
All of this may happen
without your focusing attention on it,
and some time later
you may not understand why you seem grouchy.


In the example just described, the actual effects
are likely to be of little importance
except to an entity in a sensitive state.
However, more dramatic examples would not
demonstrate the concept of
frame-by-frame-head-action observation
any better.

It is feasible for any entity
to focus attention
so closely
on one's own head action
that, experiencing the events in the previous example,
one would be totally aware
of the causes and effects at each step;

and then,
amused at one's own minor slavery to inputs,
would clear the slate of one's mind
of all the unwanted effects.


Example:

> You express a viewpoint to another entity. That entity is
> impressed. You express another viewpoint. That entity
> objects. You fast-thinkingly put together the best words
> available which will integrate your latter viewpoint
> with the objection the other entity has raised.


What has happened is that you enjoyed
impressing the other entity too much,
resulting in an insistence
on being right the second time.
Thus, you manipulated words expertly
so as to line up your own second viewpoint
with the very objection
that had been raised against it.
You did not totally reconsider your position,
taking the objection as a serious possibility;
you wanted to "win" more than you wanted truth;
you focused on word-manipulation gamesmanship
rather than on the objective,
collective search for truth.

This is common among most entities at most times.
The reward of impressing others
has not yet become boring.
As a result, most entities do not really listen
to what is said by themselves or others,
simply letting their highly-developed
word-game systems
calculate the optimum response to what has been bid,
and keeping vague track of the score.


Most of the external action taken by most entities
is of this unconsciously-motivated nature.


*the prime objective of observing head action*
*frame by frame*
*is to be able to figure out your own programmming*
*based on your actions;*
*i.e., to make conscious*
*that which is unconscious*
*or, more broadly,*
*to live in all of you simultaneously.*

Figuring out your own programming
based on your actions
is as challenging a task as,
for a computer programmer,
the task of figuring out the workings
of an extremely complex program,
based only on the reports which are output.

This is the reverse of the original process
by which you programmed yourself since birth.

In the original process,
you chose consciously which way
to act in certain circumstances
based on certain observations and logic.

That conscious logic then degraded
leaving only the predisposition
to act in similar ways from then on.


The earliest experiences you have had
have had disproportionately great programming power,
since they in effect were the groundwork,
dependent upon little prior programming;

while later experiences could have only lesser effect,
channelled
as they were
by the established
groundwork programming.


Every experience you have ever had
has programmed you in this way,
with your conscious mind
as a willing but forgetful accomplice.

When your conscious mind forgot
about why you did certain things,
you still continued to do them;

in fact, you did them with great regularity
since the conscious mind was *not able*
to interrupt or object to actions
which it had so long disregarded
as being "right" and "what I do".

*Thus, conscious or semi-conscious choices you once made
have become unconscious choices you still make today.*


*Making these conscious will allow you
to decide whether or not you want
to continue acting in the same way,*

*will expand your "youness"
to include more of you,*

*and bring more action
under control of your will.*

Example:

> You are listening to small voices in your head. You are aware that many small voices that you strain to hear are seemingly suppressed by something else in your head. You struggle to focus on the small voices, and manage to bring them to the verbal-consciousness level. At that level, you recognize them to be seemingly obvious and trivial statements which are, however, of profound relevance to you, in your situation at that moment.
>
> You note that it is "as if" there were a Stupidity Program inside your head, which was purposely attempting to drown out those important statements before you could verbalize them, therefore keeping you "stupid".

You characterize this Program as a little puppet, dancing around, distracting you, and shouting down small voices.

It occurs to you that this "Stupidity Program" is actually an "Afraid to Sound Stupid Program" which embarrassedly screens out pre-verbal ideas which seem to it, at that stage, to be obvious, trivial, naive and banal.

However,
it is characteristic of all truly important revelations
that they seem obvious,
trivial, naive and banal at first glance.

Thus such an "Afraid to Sound Stupid Program"
acts effectively to screen out self-revelation
which would otherwise immediately expose
much of the mechanical behavior
from which most entities suffer.

## *Master Meditation*

In order to foil your own
"Afraid to Sound Stupid Program",
strive to verbalize or at least visualize
all of the almost-imperceptible impulses
you detect forming in your mind
from instant to instant.


Exercise:

It is useful to set aside a regular time in which to exercise this facility in the absence of distraction.

Thus, the only subject matter on which you will have to focus is your own frame-by-frame head action;

this will gradually increase your ability to follow such action even at other times, and in the face of outside distractions.


In this self-observation period,
the greatest threat
is self-criticism.

The way this happens is as follows:

You have a thought which you are ashamed of,
because it sounds ignorant or ignoble.
You then tighten up a particular "valve"
which lets through impulses
from various hidden parts of your mind
into your conscious mind.

This creates a situation of "premature edit";
in effect, you allow the "valve"
to decide on what is worthy
of being let through.


The valve, however, makes decisions
based on the "feel"
of the nascent thought, etc.,
and is in a poor position
to select properly.

Thus, it edits out thoughts
which are couched in tentative voices,
thoughts which seem to be what they are not,
and thoughts which sound
obvious, trivial, naive or banal.

This cuts out much that should get through.

Theoretically there is no reason
why everything should not be allowed through,
in that the conscious mind
is in the best position
to evaluate and "edit"
 — i.e., discard certain thoughts —
while using others.

However, in some cases,
too much is let through,
resulting in a condition
of "Inforush Paralysis"
in which the victim
cannot handle all of the data
demanding his or her attention.

We suspect that the "valve"
is in existence
in order to guard against
"Inforush Paralysis";


but unfortunately,
as with many other aspects of consciousness
that are included for good purposes,

the "valve" is often misused,
letting too little through.

One technique for avoiding premature edit
is to write down whatever comes into your mind,

writing as quickly as possible
without reading what you are writing.

Avoid the temptation to stop
and look back at what you have written
until the flow of words itself stops
for a few moments.

It is possible, using this method,
to become single-pointed
with the attention so focused
on the little voices inside
that a trance-like state is achieved
in which the writing instrument
appears to be moving of itself,
writing words unknown.


In this state,
one runs forward
into a revelational vein,
mining deeper and deeper into the vein,
only losing track of the hinted-at next idea
when the conscious mind suddenly becomes aware
of the content which has already gone past,
and "sits up and takes notice".

This spotlight of recognition
appears to frighten the modest voices,
who seem to "zip behind trees"
when you look sharply at them.

The smallest inner voice
is that of the Master.

This is the voice of the Universe.

When you identify with this voice
your will becomes congruent
with the will of the Universe.

This is a voice incapable of giving you bad advice;
all that comes from this voice
you will instantly recognize
as clearly right
from every standpoint.


In order not to "scare away" this voice,
you must listen attentively for it,
quieting your mind;
then when you begin to hear any voices,
you must avoid the tendency
to look sharply at them
or comment on them
with your conscious mind;
imagine that you are
"looking not at them, but near them"
in order to "see" them better.

If your conscious mind
blurts out some commentary,
which is almost inevitable
for quite some time,
simply and gently quiet it
without losing your temper at yourself;
harshness or self-criticism
will also "scare away"
the Master voice.

Because of the "silent listening"
necessary to hear the Master,
it is best to have writing materials available
but not to use them at first.
The body should be parked and forgotten.*
The senses should be turned off to external reality.

The writing method described above should only be used
if the voice has been coming through
and there is no doubt anywhere in you
that what is coming through should be written down.

Again, when writing in direct response
to inner communication,
do not think about what you are writing,
do not look for opportunities to abbreviate,
or you will tend to "knock corners off"
of the pure information coming through.
Do not read the words,
worry about the spelling, meaningfulness, etc.

When the stream stops of itself
for a long enough period
that you are sure that it is a "break,"
you might look at what you have written;
this is likely to trigger a new stream, and if it does,
you should go back into "writing trance" immediately.

Continue this process
until no further information is forthcoming
or until you feel "exhausted" and satisfied
with the amount that you have to analyse.

---

*Your body and mind will tend to be most cooperative if you precede this exercise with a two-hour fast during which you enjoy a luxurious toilette and movement meditation (e.g. Hatha Yoga, etc).

When not using the writing approach,
continue to have writing materials available.

Information will tend to drift in;
you will hear a "revelation",
probably about yourself at first, or about others;
you will become excited;
moments later you will say to yourself,
"I have to remember that," or
"Wasn't that a thought!"
and will then discover
that you cannot remember the thought.

When this happens,
do not become worried;

trust the process,
and patiently wait,
knowing that the thought will return;

think about what you can remember having thought about
just before or since the missing thought,
but do so without straining to remember.

The lost thought will almost always return at once;
otherwise it will return at an appropriate later time.

*You will lose nothing forever that you need to have.*

That which you cannot get back instantaneously,
you are not yet in need of.

After recapturing a thought,
you may decide that the risk
of losing it again is too great;
or you may discover
that you have too many things
that you want to remember;
you may then decide
to suspend the "listening"
and write some things down.

In order to minimize the interruption,
do not write down whole sentences,
but merely "trigger words"
which will remind you
of particular concepts:

iceberg tips which will bring back whole icebergs.

# II.

# Transmuting Negatives Into Positives:

## *Turning Dilemma into Opportunity*

Take the best action you can
and don't worry
if your best is not good enough.

*You must play the cards
you have been dealt,
regardless of their strength,
and not bemoan your hand.*

*Bemoaning your hand
privately or publicly
merely amplifies
your so-called weaknesses,
and potentiates them
as de facto weaknesses.*

*You cannot simultaneously
bemoan your cards
and make the best of them.*

*To increase the power*
*of any hand,*

*just slightly overstate*
*the strength*
*of a weak hand*

*and just slightly understate*
*the strength*
*of a strong hand.*


**Transform worries into tasks**

**by distinguishing**
**the variables you can control**
**from the variables you cannot control;**

**then set out to control the former variables**
**and essentially ignore the latter variables.**

Worrying is negative input
once you have identified the controllable variables
and have set yourself to controlling them.


Worrying under such conditions
implies that you should concern yourself
with phenomena beyond your control;
such concern is misplaced,
since you will always have quite enough to think about
as regards phenomena that are under your control.

That which is beyond your control
is not your responsibility;

whatever happens that is beyond your control
can only be accepted as necessary.

**Correct mistakes, including your own mistakes,
without inflicting guilt on yourself or anyone else.**

You may now find that you feel guilty
whenever you find yourself thinking
in a manner you disapprove of.
This is how most individuals have been conditioned
to react to their own mistakes:

when very young, they were corrected ungently
whenever they did not follow orders properly;
until they learned all of the orders,
these ungentle corrections
occurred almost constantly.
The ungentle correction voice was then internalized
as the common model for correcting mistakes.


Individuals on the path
of consciously reprogramming themselves
will obviously need to correct their mistakes
very frequently,
and will naturally tend
to fall into the same pattern of ungentle correction
they were subjected to
in their original programming period.

This results in negative leakage of positive energies.
Energy needed for diagnosing the causes
of a particular mistake
and for generating and evaluating
alternative solutions, is wasted in internal threats
and punches and screams at oneself.

*These energies are not merely wasted, however,
since energy expressed negatively
programs you and the environment
to bring about still more negative occurrence.*

*When you catch yourself in a mistake,
seek to understand why you did it.*

Decide on a proper policy for the next time
a similar situation arises,
so that you can realistically expect
not to make the same mistake again.


Know that there is no catching yourself in mistakes
unless you have already made enough conscious progress
to spot needed revisions in your programming;

thus, be thankful that you are catching yourself
in mistakes.


Catching yourself in mistakes is a sign
that you are in transition between behavior patterns.

Know that if you make a mistake and *catch yourself,*
the net of these two things is positive:

therefore be happy
at finding yet another course-correction.


*Know that mistakes and negative events
are necessary to progress;*

like a vaccine,
they stimulate the production of antitoxins
in the form of revised programming
now capable of dealing with similar threats in the future.

If your experience is untroubled,
you will never develop the means
to deal with troubling experience.

Therefore, focus on the ultimate goals,
and be thankful for any experience
which brings you closer to these,

whether the experience itself
be seemingly positive or negative.


If you hear a voice in your head
harshly reprimanding you for a mistake,
disidentify with that voice.

Say: "Program, your intentions are good,
but you are not being helpful."

Think of this program as a base
that has been planted in your mind
by every harsh teacher, relative or peer
that ever sought to program you;

an automatic message sender activated
to scream its one message at you
whenever you err.

Look at every mistake and negative experience
as a valued teacher,
an opportunity which opens to maximum limits
the possibilities for your future
by showing you new choices.

Ask yourself: "What has been honed by this?"

You may find after your severest mistakes
that you now have sufficient motivation
to carry out a change
that you have wanted to make for some time
but lacked sufficient impetus.

*Mistakes are the impetus
which actualize your free will,
just as a spring gains its energy by being crushed.*

Emphasize *doing your best* rather than succeeding.

It is not important that you ever live
in an error-free manner,
but that you move toward freeing yourself
of inappropriate programming.

Therefore consider that all mistakes you make
occur during your trial period,
when you are allowed to make mistakes
so that you can learn from them.

All of the foreseeable future is your trial period:
the playing-for-score never begins.
Therefore avoid being a scorekeeper:
neither give nor remove points from your score.

*Experience is to provide
learning and happiness,
not points.*

Accept negative emotion as a useful sign
but set to work on converting the sign
into complete understanding.

Regard the emotion you feel as communication to you
from an inner part of yourself
that is acutely sensitive but inarticulate.

Neither fear nor dread this useful sign
as an agony or punishment,
or as an indication of your own weakness,
incompleteness or fallibility:

negative emotion is as necessary
a warning system as physical pain.


However, it would be as inappropriate
to submit to negative emotion
as it would be to submit to pain:

*the clear course of action*
*is to understand*
*and thereby remove negative emotion.*

Do not waste energy
on negative feelings or morbid thoughts.

Your feelings and thoughts program
you and your environment on many levels:

if you radiate negatively,
negative events will occur around you and to you;

the opposite will occur if you radiate positively.

**Transform negative inputs into positive outputs.**

**Find and exploit the positive aspects of every thing.**

**Hesitate to conclude that a thing or event
is either good or bad.**

Much that seems bad serves good purpose.
When some thing or event seems bad to you,
ask yourself:
"Might this be viewed
as happening for some good purpose?"
and seek to discover
what such a good purpose might be.

This potentially has the power of programming you
and others around you
to turning the event to such good purpose.

You have the power to experience anything as good,
by perceiving it as such;

this is not illusion because goodness and badness
have no independent existence apart from
your having ascribed them to things.

Thus, seek the good in what is given,
and seek to do good in what you control.


Be happy with whatever is happening
unless there is strong evidence
that something else should be happening.

**Take everything that happens
as potentially constructive communications to you
from somewhere,**
and figure out what you have to do
to get maximum positive value
out of these events/communications.


Do not underrate your ignorance
as compared to what
an omniscient universe might know;

thus, do not look at a situation and hastily conclude
that it is "bad".


Introduce your own changes in a situation cautiously,

and be aware
of the potential hidden value already present
in any situation,
regardless of appearances.

If bothered, seek isolation.

Plan to be uninterrupted for several hours.
Then confront what is bothering you slowly,
inspecting each aspect of it.

Know that this condition
is because you have adopted an inflexible position
that may or may not be appropriate.

Seek to find out what that position is,
and decide on its appropriateness.


                You have probably been conditioned to think,
                        in conflicts between individuals,
                              of one party as being "right"
                                and the other as being "wrong".

                this way of thinking is counterproductive
                      in that it motivates you to not want
                          to be the party who is "wrong".

                thus, you may tend to bend over backwards
                      to maintain your original "rightness".

## *What would happen if you just yielded to the bothersome situation?*

Imagine how this yielding might take place,
and how you might rearrange other thoughts
so that your new situation
would accommodate everything comfortably.

Know that you have probably been conditioned
to think of yielding as defeat;
this is inappropriate.

It may seem to be bending away
from one's own motivations,
but actually turn out to be the useful opportunity
for inspection and refinement
of one's motivations.

You are not the entity
that controlled your body a short time ago;
be willing to criticize the previous administration.

**Yielding is the bending
in the specific direction required
to release the tension.**

*Remember that all rightness and wrongness,
like goodness and badness,
is ascribed,
and is not resident in any event or thing.*

Be aware that the goal in any inter-entity conflict
should be truth,
and not superiority.


Remember that your success
is not dependent
on the success of the robot
you currently inhabit;

if it must be sacrificed
because of a prior mistake,
prepare yourself to go on without it,
but seek to understand which actions
were mistaken.

Know further that in virtually
all inter-entity conflicts,
admission of a mistake of any magnitude
rarely requires sacrifice
of the current robot.

Do not visualize other entities
as having power over you;

**instead, see that all entities
are the same one
looking out at itself
through various windows.**

In this context,
the superiority of one window
over another
is obviously meaningless.

*Cooperate with all other windows in seeking truth,
and accept mistakes by any window including your own
as the necessary learning experiences that they are.*


Strive to see all the implications of a situation.
Set closure way back.
Do not accept the things that you say to yourself
until supported by evidence
you can present to yourself.

On issues lacking evidence,
reserve judgment.

Learn to tolerate suspension of belief
one way or the other
on issues requiring more information;

otherwise you will make decisions on all issues,
regardless of the scarcity of your information.


Avoid decisions until they are necessary,
and define information needed
to aid in proper decision-making;
then seek such information.

*If you find yourself bothered*
*and in a situation*
*in which you are taking*
*whatever happens or is said*
*in a negative light,*

*seek isolation and rest your mind.*

*Solutions and release may be presented to you.*


Accept deprivation;
to do otherwise is to accept slavery to desire.

Know that, once deprived,
your next experience of the thing desired
will be so much more intense
as to more than compensate for the deprivation.

There is no motivation without deprivation,

no appreciation without motivation,

and thus no appreciation without deprivation.

Imagine that the universe is a grand hotel
in which the waiters are continually bringing you
new and exotic foods to sample;

how inappropriate it would be
to refuse some strange-looking platters
and demand only to be given
the same plate as yesterday.


*Change is necessary to evolution;*
the universe contains incredible diversity
and you cannot experience it all
within the confines of one comfortable life style.


Look ahead to what you will think
of your life at its end;
you will probably not want to look back
and say that it was cozy and dull.

Thus, react positively to what seems to be disaster.

*Remember that what seems now to be disaster*
*may be an important step toward evolution,*
*and may even be identifiable as such*
*at some point in the future.*

Every great loss takes you out of a rut
and starts your life anew;
be grateful for the time you had
in your former happy state
and look forward eagerly
to the new phase.

Play life as a game;

play as well as you can;
end the game when this is preferable;

until that point,
recognize that you are playing the game
out of choice and preference.


Learn to laugh at adversity,
for it is the fuel of evolution.

Learn to laugh at the universe's jokes.

Accept the tragicomic aspect of your life
as an essential element in its being interesting.

Knowing that diverse inputs
stimulate creativity,
look at each annoying disturbance
as a diverse input.


Know that another ambush along this path
is a feeling of emptiness or boredom
which can occur at moments
when you realize that every problem is under control.

This occurs so rarely in normal existence
that one is unprepared for it.

To deal with this ambush,
recognize it as the invitation
to a new phase of consciousness:

*accept emptiness,*

*maintain concentration on emptiness,*

*and see what happens.*


Learn to accept an emotionally neutral state
as happiness.

You have probably been conditioned
to think of happiness
as euphoria;
this is inappropriate.

Expect voices in your head
to tell you that you are in
a bad mood
when you are merely non-euphoric;

tell these voices that they may be
in a bad mood,
but you are not.

*Remember: you are not the chatter
that you hear in your head;
you are the hearer of that chatter.*

Expect only that existence will be interesting,
and you will be happy.

Expect that you will be happy per se,
and anything less than perfect ecstasy
will be a bitter disappointment.

Do not be disturbed by the discovery
of impure thoughts in your head.

You did not originate any of these thoughts,
nor did you seek to have them put into your head.

Your effort to prevent them from erupting
into inappropriate action
is fully meeting your responsibility
with regard to these thoughts.

The presence of these thoughts in your head,
buffered by your free will
from becoming actualized,
is necessary to the comprehensiveness
of your information file;

if you did not have these thoughts,
you could not fully understand
others with these thoughts.

Not understanding them,
you could not forgive them.

Not forgiving them,
you could not love them.

Not loving them,
you could not be them.

Not being them, **you would continue your present amnesia
in which you think that you are the robot
you currently inhabit.**

Know that there may be times
when you find yourself
both fascinated and terrified
by morbid imaginings, premonitions of doom,
or waking nightmares.

These may have a number of different sources:

they may be produced by a unique interaction
of chemicals in the body;

they may be communications from other minds,
stored or direct;

they may be communications from yourself
for the purpose of testing reactions.


Such temporary fixations are given some credibility
when one's existence has been positive
for a period of time;
one begins to wonder
when the inevitable tragedy will strike.

Further seeming credibility is added by the recognition
that strange and unpredictable trivial accidents
are happening all the time;
*this suggests that a strange and unpredictable*
*tragic accident is overdue.*

Actually, this generalization
from the trivial to the tragic
is a non sequitur.

Under such conditions, take the following action:

Imagine the worst so as to be prepared to face it;
but do not assume that the worst will occur
or has occurred.

Defuse the emotion involved
by being prepared to face the feared situation
in reality.

**Worry is highly correlated with the awareness
that one doesn't know what one will do
in the feared situation.**

Estimate the probability,
based on past experience
and all other information available,
that the feared situation will come to pass
during a specific period of time.
In virtually all cases,
this probability will be exceedingly low.

Decide, based on the probabilities,
whether to bet that the disaster will strike,
or make the opposite bet.

Look closely
to see the vague nightmare images in your mind.

Are they faces?
Specific types of events?
Specific facial expressions?
Sounds?

Focus on remembering
where you may have first seen these images,
and where you have seen these images since.

Pinpoint the communications
in which these images have been suggested to you.

Seek to understand
why these images seem frightening to you.


In many cases, these may be images
presented to you as frightening
when you were very young;
you may accept them as frightening
for this reason only.


Remember that there is nothing to fear;
that you decide what you want to avoid,
and can best avoid these things
without fearing them.

Be sympathetic to your fear-images;
imagine that it is hurtful to them
to be so intensely rejected by you.

Resolve to help your fear-images
find a happy home in your head;
greet them warmly whenever they return.

Remember that they are
just other types of things
to look at.


**Always assume that there is some way out
of a "bad" situation,
and your object is to find that way.**

**In this way, you exercise your will
by always assuming that it has a vehicle.**

Thus, focus on finding the way out,
not on suffering from the fear
that there is no way out.
The "way out" will always be the one way
which allows you to turn the bad situation
into something useful:

in effect, the bad situation
has been set up
so that you could learn
how to convert it into good.


Thus, ask yourself:

*"What is the brighter side of this?"* and

*"Where in this mess lies the opportunity?"*

Example #1:

> You find that you have fear. You take this to be a "bad" situation, and you are negative about it.
>
> You then realize that your emotions are contacting you to tell you something.
>
> You then work on the message and decipher it to be: "Be alert".
>
> You have decoded the original intent of the fear, i.e., to make yourself alert to possible danger;
>
> you have converted negative fear to positive alertness.
>
> This can only come about
> by confronting your own fear
> and the reasons for it,
> and what you can do about it;
> and what you can't do about it;
>
> then taking the action that is takeable
> and ignoring that which is beyond your control.

Example #2:

> You find that you have made a mistake. You take this to be a "bad" situation, and are negative about it. You then realize that your emotions are telling you something by means of this negativity; i.e., to learn what to do differently so that you do not make the same mistake again in a similar situation.

You think about and learn this:
the negative emotion goes away;
you have converted it
into what it was intended to convey
when it was sent to you
from your emotion-creator.

Example #3:

> You find that you are having your first setback in a particular project. You take this to be a "bad" situation, a turning-about of a good streak. You then realize that the setback might be a useful learning experience out of which can come new strength; that the smoothness with which the project had been going might have been a bit understimulating; that conquering the setback will be an exciting challenge which will result in the minimizing of the possibility for similar setbacks in the future, at which point they might be more dangerous. You say excitedly to a friend: "I'm having my first setback on project X!"

You have converted the setback into strength.
Bear in mind that strength cannot exist
without resistance.

Example #4:

> You find that you feel inferior in a specific situation; you interpret this to be a message to you to compensate for the inferiority you feel by getting angry at anything in the universe which would have you feel inferior to it.
>
> You then moderate this anger by realizing that the others whom you are using to make yourself feel inferior are not fully aware of what they are doing, and are doing it out of their own weakness in any case.
>
> The anger, moderated, becomes aggressive determination not to be put down;
>
> this is precisely what was needed in the situation, and this was the reason your emotions sent you the feeling of inferiority;
>
> to stimulate a compensatory set.

# 12.

## Visualizing the Whole Universe As One Thing:

## Identifying With All You Perceive

*Visualize the whole universe as one thing:*
*every individual of every species,*
*every idea,*
*every event,*
*every moment of time,*
*every percept,*
*every lump of matter and energy:*
*all parts of one thing.*

This is either the way it is,
or one valid way of looking at it,
or a useful fiction.

It is useful to look at it this way,
because it then becomes possible
to gradually identify your consciousness
with that of the whole universe.

This shift in consciousness
is facilitated
by visualizing the universe as one thing.

Know that if the universe is one thing,
those individuals who see themselves
as separate from the totality
are **deluded;**

such individuals comprise
the bulk of your species.

However, from time to time,
two or more individuals recognize each other,
as being one thing together.

When this recognition is sensed emotively,
we call this **love;**

when this recognition is sensed cognitively,
we call this expansion of consciousness
or **telepathy.**

This recognition occurs as if the universe,
having forgotten that it is one thing
and having fragmented into billions
of individual consciousnesses,

is more or less dimly recognizing its identity.

Thus, when two individuals fall in love
it is as if two fragments
of the universal consciousness
have remembered that

they are one.

To the extent of their love,
they will cease to seek individual goals,
and will begin to seek mutual goals.

Two consciousnesses seeking mutual goals
are in the process of gradually
becoming aware of themself
as one consciousness.

Once the goals are merged,
the perceptions and memories
are in a position to follow.

*Know that the purpose of love*

*is to reunite the universal consciousness.*

## *Nobility:*

Pretend always that you are the whole universe,
and not merely the one individual whose body
you currently seem to occupy.

Thus you will tend to identify
with the goals of the universe
and not merely with the goals
of one individual.

As a result, you will feel
justified in treating
all individuals equally,
including the individual
through whose eyes you currently peek.

This is the meaning of the metametaprogram

*"Treat others as you treat yourself"*;

in effect, these others are to be seen as your self;
every object in the universe
is to be seen as your self.


When you feel that you as an individual
have failed or are in danger,
remind yourself that the fate of the one cog
that is your current link to this plane
is trivial;

*your concern is with the progress
of the whole you,
the whole universe.*

Do not be overly concerned with the robot
through whom you currently act;
statistically, it is unlikely
to be the greatest or the lowest;

its successes and failures
are microscopic and fleeting at best.


Do not be overly impressed or depressed by your robot;
it is not necessarily your only agent on this plane;
nor is it necessarily your first or last vehicle.

Consider it only as one of your more controllable,
and therefore one of your more useful,
tools on this plane.


Know that as you expand your identification
from your current robot to include others around you,
loved ones, other species, inanimate objects,
and eventually the entire universe,

your control sphere similarly expands.


However, this does not happen if it is your objective.

If your motives are truly "the good of all",
this will be sensed by others
and they will cooperate with you,
lending their energies to your actions.

If your motives are to simulate selflessness
in order to gain power for your self,
this will be sensed by others
and they will tend to not cooperate with you,
lending their energies to the muffling of your actions.


In effect,
as a sector of the universe recognizes itself
it begins to act concertedly,
with the force of all of its components combined.


*If you work for the good of the whole universe,
the whole universe will work with you.*


This benefit does not depend upon your belief
in the metaphysical reality
of the oneness of the universe;

that is why we suggest that you adopt
the viewpoint of the universe
regardless of your beliefs

regarding the nature of reality.

Imagine that the universe has a plan
for what events should take place
at which times
so that consciousness evolves fully and merges.


If you then line up your motives
with those of the universe,
your job is obviously

to follow the universe's plan.


Since that plan is not written down anywhere,
your best clue as to what the plan is,
is "that which happens".


                        Learn to distinguish

                        between the times
                        when you should
              "flow with" the universe's plan,

                    and the times
      when you should exercise your own will.

              When others around you
           seek to make things happen,
        and you feel essentially neutral,
             "flow with" the universe;
        otherwise your cog may be
banged around by stronger machinery.

When you feel uncomfortable
with what others ask of you,
find a way to absent yourself
physically or mentally
long enough
to diagnose what is happening
and what you should do.


Never do something for someone else
unless you can do it freely;

otherwise you are not treating yourself
as well as you treat others,
and the net value to the universe
is actually being reduced
by your selflessness.


Beware of compromises in which
one side still harbors doubts;
the only successful solutions are those
in which all sides gain.

All other solutions will come undone,
with net cumulative loss to the universe.


Know that causation involves responsibility.


You are responsible for whatever causal contribution
will have been made
by all of the occasions
on which you exert your will
rather than simply flowing with the universe.

A total "flowing with" implies
that you are merely a passive medium
through which causes flow unchanged.


Obviously, whenever you are not certain
that you are acting properly,
you will want to "flow with"
whatever is happening

so as not to assume responsibility
for imprudent actions.


Be careful of every word and facial gesture
you make in communicating:

those who are listening or watching
may be influenced in their lives'
most important decisions.

This applies much more strongly
when young minds are around
to be influenced;

their relatively vacant memories

amplify

causality.

When individuals seem to differ,
and one of those individuals
is your current robot,
decide what action to take
giving equal consideration to all individuals.


In other words,
treat others no better and no worse
than you treat your current robot.

Do not sacrifice your current robot
to the whims of others,

and do not sacrifice others
to the whims of your current robot.


    Decide proper action based on the criterion

    of maximizing the net value to all concerned.

    For example, sacrificing your entire life
    for one other person would seem to result
    in losses merely equalizing gains
    for the universe;

    however,
    sacrificing ten minutes of your life
    for someone else's hour gained
    would seem to result
    in more gains than losses
    for the universe.

Do not create unnatural pockets of acceptance
in the universe.


That is, do not go along with others
just to be kind,
when their actions discomfit you;

this would have the effect
of reinforcing such actions
so that they will tend to be repeated
more frequently and intensively.


> Your cog is where it is
> to naturally buffer other cogs
> so that the whole machine
> sticks to the plan.
>
> Let your cog
> be explicitly honest
> with the other cogs.
>
> However, despite the immense power
> of the huge driving wheels
> of the universe,
>
> ultimately the smallest gears
> are delicately balanced,
>
> and so always compound
> your honesty with gentleness.

Do not act in uncertainty when considering others.

Unless you are certain of what they desire,
and of the strength of their desire,
do not seek to "act considerately".

Otherwise you may be wasting energy
in actions unrelated to, or counter to
their real desires.

Invest some energy
in researching their motives
before committing too much energy
to serving their supposed motives.

Ultimately, decide what to do
considering not merely them
but everyone else as well.


The amount of information you collect before action
should be proportional
to the importance of the decision.

In trivial matters,
you can gauge the strength of other's desires
by careful observation
of their face, tone of voice,
or other such manifestations if any.

In more important matters,
direct questions have no substitute.

**Do not be critical of that which has happened;**

do decide what should have happened
and seek to bring it about
in similar situations in the future.

What has already happened
could not have been otherwise;
all events are merely the resultant of their causes,
which are themselves events
dependent on the constellation of prior causes.

You can make yourself a more potent cause
of future events
by deciding how to act differently
the next time the same kind of situation arises;

you can do nothing about the past.


Do not be critical of what any individual
including yourself,
has done:
all actions are merely the resultant of their causes.

Again, seek only to set new policies
for similar future situations.

Honesty and gentleness
are essential tools
in this endeavor.

Guiding others to adopt
more useful new policies
requires special gentleness;

often it is best to simply ask the right questions
to have the desired effect.

Be wary of the tendency to see flaws in other entities;

this is a common pattern
for those on the path
of self-observation.


As you critically review your own
internal and external behavior,

you will also tend to
automatically do the same
for the observed behavior of others.

While it is your right
to change your own programming,
it is not your right
to unilaterally change or wish to change another's.


Thus, it is inappropriate to "note desired changes",
i.e., to "react critically".

It is appropriate to accept
the behavior of others
(i.e., of the total environment
not under your current control)
as given, and therefore as
neither good nor bad.

Seek to change only
that which cries out for change
within yourself,

and to a much lesser extent,
that which is outside yourself
which the universe
appears to be asking you to change.

More than this is meddlesome.


Remember that your view of the universe's plan
is necessarily limited at most times,

and so what you think of as an evil
may be in fact a necessary learning stimulus
for an individual or species.


Thus do not strive to combat evil
except when the universe cues you
that this is your role in the plan.

Thus, do not give advice
unless it is asked for or cued
by the situation
in a way which your inner senses
will gradually be able to identify.


Do not be critical of those on other paths
who seem to have progressed less
in specific problem areas:

*they are where they should be now
in the universal plan.*

Nor feel superior to such individuals,
for the net balance
of each entity's worth
to the universe
*is always* 1:

that which you supply by your cleverness
or purity of intent
is not more valuable to the universe
than another's all-consuming passion
or single-minded submission
to conditioning:

*in the viewpoint of creation,*
*all of these brushstrokes*
*are aesthetically pleasing*
*and necessary.*


**Forgive all by understanding all.**

Understanding all
involves appreciating all of the causes.

An individual may do a wrong action,
but that action
in the individuals's mind
is always supported
by a chain of reasoning
which validly reflects the assumptions


that individual has been forced to
by his or her experiences.

If you do not yet forgive an individual,
it is because you do not yet understand it;

you have not yet allowed yourself
to look out from its eyes
and appreciate
its chain of reasoning;

you are not looking at things
the way the universe does;

you are looking out from partisan eyes.


To forgive a person,

for a time in your imagination,

be that person.



*To forgive all,*
*be all.*

# Practical Application

### *Creating an Untouchable Spacetime*

Let's say you have a gallon of attention.

Under normal circumstances,
you are probably someplace where you can see and hear
other human beings.
Human beings generate very nonrandom sounds and sights
for your brain to decode.
Being anywhere you can see or hear one
takes at least a quart of attention out of your gallon,
whether you think you are "paying attention to them"
or not.

(We don't always know how much of our attention
something is taking.
Only if we are very conscious will we realize
that our thought processes seem slowed down,
senses are dulled, grace of movement is impaired,
and so on.
Then we may realize that the cause of it is a distraction
of some parts of the Self which seem more interested
in monitoring other humans
than in one's own mentation,
whatever it may be at the moment.

These parts which are more interested in other people
than in your thoughts,
are your emotional and physical centers.
They are distinctly anti-intellectual
and so find it difficult at the best of times
to stay attentive to inner council sessions,
let alone when they begin to resonate
at emotional-physical levels
with others of the same species.

Thus, if you are to be with your Self
with all parts fully attending,
you must be some place
where you are not able to perceive other human beings.)


Going back to our "normal circumstances":

you've already lost a quart
out of your gallon of attention,
to other humans around you.

Next is another quart at least
for the "recorded" thoughts in your head —
that is, thoughts which have come up before
without resolution,
and which now come up only to trigger a chain
of rapid electrochemical events,
which, essentially, just change the subject.
This normal bath of "repeater thoughts"
is usually going on and taking its quart of attention.

Then let us say
that you are not in the most comfortable position.
Perhaps you are cutting off your own circulation somewhere,
or keeping your muscles unnecessarily tense somewhere,
or your clothes are too tight somewhere, etc.
This will take almost another quart of attention,
even if you are totally unaware of it.
And if there was a fly in the room,
you might have none left at all!

The significance of this long-winded
"gallons and quarts" analogy
is that in order to reach the levels of being
which are your birthright,
you need consistent use
of very nearly *the full gallon* of attention:
even *an ounce or two* slipping away to other distractions
prevents you from reaching your goal!

(You might think of this as a kind of "critical mass"
necessary to trigger the "atomic chain reaction"
in your Self:
one neutron short and it doesn't go.)

        For now, accept this as our assertion and later on
                you will see that it is true.

## *Ideal Conditions*

Eventually you will find that it is essential
to have at least one hour every day
during which *no distraction can get to you.*

With experience you will know
that the *clarity* with which you can perceive the world
from this vantage point
is not possible under any other conditions.
(Your "full gallon of attention" cannot be kept together
under any other conditions.)


The best setting for your "alone space"
is amidst Nature —
sitting in it, hearing it, smelling it, seeing it —
with no other humans in view or likely to happen by.
The sound of ocean or stream is especially conducive
to the higher states.

In many cases, however,
you will have to settle for the indoors.
Then you'll need a room with a door
and the oral equivalent
of a "Please Do Not Disturb" sign.

Roommates are sometimes frightened
when asked "not to disturb" at certain times.
Thus it would be best to put it to them
in a gentle, reasonable way.
(You might let them read these pages.)
Don't be surprised if they ask for their own "alone space"
pretty soon thereafter.

Yet another alternative is the bathtub.
This is especially conducive to the higher states
both because the comfort factor removes "body noise"
and *water ionization improves intuitive receptivity.* \*

If not in the bathtub,
be conscious about putting your body in positions
in which it will like to stay for long periods
without continuously flashing grievance messages.

Be conscious about sounds reaching you,
especially sounds of human activity.
If this is getting through the walls,
some soft instrumental nonsentimental music
could be used as a sonic shield.
Indian ragas, Bach,
whatever doesn't bring your mind down to mundane levels,
and which keeps out extraneous noise.

           Follow your intuition in setting up these conditions.
                  Don't push where there is strain.
                      Go the easy way at first.
            Later you can gradually get closer to the ideal.

---

\* Hypothesis for validation.

## *How to Use these Periods*

These are times for you to *be*
with your Self.

Do whatever *you* —
all parts of you together —
want to do most at that moment.


The point, however, is not for you to distract your Self
with television, radio or reading.
Do these at other times.
These are analogous to bringing back other human beings
in some form.

Do not answer telephone calls at these times,
if at all possible.


        *Be* with

        your Self.


        Just try it.

## *How Was That?*

Interestingly, often what a person will want to do first
when alone with the Self (after making it comfortable)
is to make a list of things, or several lists.

These will be lists that have been "on the Self's mind",
and when you stop "running",
to listen to the Self for a while,
the first thing it does is unload its notes.
There is always a remarkable feeling of release
once these have been transferred to paper.

Almost anything you put on paper
during your "alone spaces"
is worth keeping for a while.
Best to date everything, keep it in order,
look back over it from time to time,
throw out stuff taken care of already
(or put it in the Archives).

Some of these are simply notes to do chores.
Others are longstanding problems which seem insoluble.
Some are things we want to think about more
in order to understand them better.

It's always helpful to sort one's lists
into categories like these.

## "One Fresh Thought on the Matter Each Time"

It can be frustrating
to look at a list of longstanding problems
you don't know how to solve.

One way of reducing the frustration
is to realize that it comes from *impatience*.
Deep down inside, on longstanding problems,
one usually realizes that whatever the solution
it is likely to involve long, hard effort.
This plus the complexity of the situation
is so discouraging that one becomes fixated
on "easy solutions",
and then refuses to even begin
to think about all the complexities
and how to untangle them:
the mind is "set" to only want to see "easy solutions".

                                        The way out of this loop
is to have just *one* "fresh thought on the matter"
each time you reconsider a situation.
That way you are not pressing for ultimate solutions
immediately;
you are merely pursuing step-by-step progress.
The part of the mind that insists on an easy solution,
usually sees this as a reasonable compromise.

Note that this creative compromise
transmutes the energy
which usually is expressed as "frustration"
so that it instead manifests as "progress".

## *Babbling & Energy Use in General*

Stay conscious of your gallon of attention.
It's your conscious energy; your creative energy.
It's the best stuff you've got;
because with it you can get anything else,
and without it you can't get anything.
It's your free will, potentially.

If there's one thing worth hoarding, it's your attention.

Yet human beings have generally not discovered this,
and squander their attention in many ways.
Chief among these is babbling,
both to oneself and to others.

"Babbling" is defined as *unnecessary communication*.

The exciting thing about babbling
is that it represents a watershed of energy
available to you if you stop babbling.

"Stopping babbling" is an interesting process.
One discovers how little control one has
over one's actions.
Somehow "the robot" keeps babbling.

This is good, because it helps identify
that *there is a robot there*,
*a thing apart from Your Own True Will*.

You will find that it is this robot
which is wasting all your energy.
Somehow it has never forgotten anything it's heard,
and has taken much of it to heart
with the force of post-hypnotic suggestion:
now it has an opinion it needs to express on every issue,
and somehow it needs to keep moving continuously,
doing hosts of priority trivia,
of importance to some nitpick circuits in your brain.

You have "reclaimed your castle"
when the robot lets you do exactly as you please.
This is a very gradual process; and we are into it here.

# *Debabblation*

### Outer Debab

When you have an impulse to say something to someone,
hear it in your *head*
and foresee/feel the mutual reaction,
while you check in your *heart*
whether it's "necessary communication" or "babble"
to your judgment.
If both the foreseeing/hearing/feeling
and the judgment feel good,
go ahead instantly without hesitation.
Otherwise wait
until the other person brings that subject up.


This procedure becomes automatic,
takes less than a second,
and can cut babble a lot.
It should not be followed mechanically,
but creatively adapted
to individual style and circumstances.

## Inner Debab

There is an automatic compulsion
to talk out in words to oneself
the ideas one has just had,
even though one knows what is going to be said
before it is said.
This is actually a form of gloating, as well as babble.

This talking out in words
of something you already know
without an explicit reason for doing so
wastes energy *and*
*traps you in last second's perspective.*
Momentarily immobilizes your mind. Kills its momentum.


If you catch yourself chattering on the intercom,
just trail off emotionlessly and quite guiltlessly
and go on to the reality at hand.

No matter how often this happens,
keep up the procedure.
Don't let the robot wear you down! Or make you mad!
It's a long ride,
but you tame the robot in the end!

*Since your mind goes faster than words,*
*why use them in your mind?*

## *Attitude Toward Time*

There never seems to be enough time
to do everything that seems to have to get done.

This is because the mind gets robotically locked into
"having to do" all at once,
all of the things it foresees possibly wanting to do
in the near future.
The thing to do is to maintain a continuously-updated
list of what has to get done (i.e. a future calendar),
pushing things back as far in time as they can go
without paying a cost you don't want to pay.
Leaving you free in the NOW to do *whatever* you want —
including starting on the one thing
that you've just set back in time
that *you* really *want* to work on *now*,
if it turns out that way.

Whenever new input comes in,
integrate it in this calendar on a priority basis
before setting to work on it, if possible.


In this way, endeavor to always keep the present moment
free of time pressure
(which otherwise takes too many pints of attention
away from you).

## What if There Is Objective Time Pressure?

Sometimes the Universe presents us
with temporary emergency conditions,
during which it is our job to do many things
in a short period of time.
When this happens,
it will not be possible to maintain an undisturbed NOW
for more than the hour or so each day
of untouchable spacetime.
During the rest of the time,
events will press in
and there will be continual decisions to be made.

In such times,
the same calendar procedure works even better.
You will probably get swamped each day
and have to update the calendar each night.
But this means you will still know the total plan
before sleep,
which will refine it for you by morning.

You will find that losing track of the calendar
for more than a day at a time,
invariably allows the feeling of time pressure
to come back into your consciousness
and rob you of attention.
If everything you have to do is on a calendar
by the end of each day,
you can go through periods of objective time pressure
without the distracting and enervating *feeling*
of time pressure,
i.e. with full effectiveness.

## Chinese Finger Trap

Impatience
comes about
when we are childishly unable to wait
("Are we there yet, Mommy?
I want to BE THERE NOW!
I wannit! I wannit! Wahhhh...")
for the future conditions
that we are working toward
to arrive.

When impatience arises,
it always delays
these future conditions we desire.

                        The only way to bring the future closer
                            is to make the BEST of the NOW.

# Twice-a-Day Tuneups

Almost everyone recognizes the need
for some physical exercise.
There are many methods and each has its proponents.

The stretching postures we recommend
are more beneficial
than any set of general physical exercises
devised by the current culture;
they were identified as being of optimal real value
over thousands of years
of rigorous scientific observation,
by people of unimpeachable integrity.

These stretching postures are, of course, Hatha Yoga.

In a way, they are more of an "inner massage"
than they are "physical exercises".
One doesn't huff and puff, and sweat, and drive oneself
to greater and greater peaks of exertion.
In effect, a giant hand comes down
and flexes the body in certain body-wise ways
(the way cats know exactly how to ripple-stretch)
which squeeze various substances through inner passages
and press tensions out of every nerve, muscle,
organ and skin cell.

Instantly there is a rush of cerebro-spinal fluid
through the brain and spinal cord.
This manifests as sparklingly clarified perceptions,
elevated mood, serene confidence,
body comfort, and so on.

Note: There are many fine hatha yoga books and thousands of capable instructors. A good place to start for a gentle stretch routine is with John Friend's video "Yoga for Meditators." For an excellent overview and pictorial study of hatha yoga, try *Yoga: The Iyengar Way*, by Silva Mehta. These can be followed up by more in-depth study with B. K. S. Iyengar's books.

## Foods & Sleep

Eat very consciously and slowly,
under the most peaceful conditions possible.
If you eat as consciously as possible
you will be able to trust your body
to tell you what to eat.
You may not necessarily be able to trust it yet
as to quantity, however:
so stay consciously committed
to the principle of moderation.

As you begin to eat more consciously,
you will probably find yourself
demanding better quality foods.
These may sometimes be more costly,
but nourishment per dollar will increase,
and quantity may decrease, to offset this.

These will tend to be foods which are fresher,
less processed,
and containing fewer artificial ingredients.
You may find yourself shifting more
toward fruits and vegetables,
fish and fowl, and better meats less frequently;
and away from poorer quality meats,
snacks and sweets, canned goods.
If you don't notice this pattern, don't worry about it;
it will happen when the time comes.

Eat when you are hungry, if the timing is right.
If you do this, you may find that you "naturally" eat
more than three times a day, but less at each sitting.

Similarly, sleep when you are sleepy,
if the timing is right.
If you do this, you may find that you "naturally" sleep
more than once a day, but less overall.

## Fear & Anger

Fear and anger help make the body tense.

The proper use of fear and anger is to get their message
and "turn off the alarm".

When you feel fear, this is to get you to realize
what it is that you are frightened of,
so that you resign your Self to it "if it happens"
(this turns off the fear-alarm)
and begin to take steps to minimize
the chance of it happening,
if that is what you then decide to do.
*You cannot effectively take these steps*
*if you forget to turn off the fear-alarm.*
Thus a useful sense becomes a danger
if there is not knowledge of its proper use.

When you feel anger,
this is to get you to realize
what it is that you are attached to,
which you are frightened of losing,
that is making you angry;
so that you resign your Self to losing it "if it happens"
(this turns off the anger-alarm)
and begin to take steps to minimize
the chances of such loss,
if that is what you then decide to do.
*You cannot effectively take these steps*
*if you forget to turn off the anger-alarm.*
Thus a useful sense becomes a threat
if there is not understanding of its proper use.

An operational definition of an *adult* is:
someone able to regularly apply the above information,
whether or not consciously aware of it.

## *Breathing & Relaxing*

At almost any moment you check your body,
you're likely to find muscles tight
where they don't have to be,
and breathing shallow as if constricted.

Keeping muscles unnecessarily tight
takes a quart of attention,
although you don't notice.
Breathing too shallowly means
that you are taking less oxidation energy than you could —
why do that?

You need all the energy you can get
for *your* real priorities:
don't let the robot fritter away
or turn away any of this energy *you* need,
with habitual tendencies to be tense.

                              Remember to relax and breathe.

# Outroduction

Imagine...

a guy sitting at his desk,
lingering over morning coffee,
feet up on the desk.

"Gee, I'd better get to work," he thinks.

Another voice in his mind then says:

"Where is that impulse coming from?
If the universe
(as represented by My Own True Will)
wants me to get to work,
that's one thing —
but, is it just my desperate ego programming
that's driving me away from lingering in this blissful
moment?"


Voicelessly, the mind of this person drifts backward
and becomes conscious
of looking at the first two voices
as separate from itself.
Without words, it is implying

"Look at those two guys fighting in there."

The man at his desk smiles,
still totally relaxed —
no muscles tightened
even at the "get to work" thought.

The man is pleased with himself
for not having gotten attached
to the inner debate.

"But maybe I'm really fooling myself
into shirking actual duty
that others need me to be doing right now?"

a mental voice suddenly asks,
flashing an image of Ulysses' men
laid out under trees snoozed out on lotus drug.


This raises so many questions
in the mind
that none of them get verbalized.

If the man was running in EOP* at this point,
there would be an unpleasant dissonance experienced,
and the man would probably find himself
jerked into a sitting position;

he would get to work in a somewhat dissociated fashion,
catch himself in some simple mistake,
and then really stop and think
about work to be done —

totally forgetting
the subject of the mini-debate
whose dissonance mechanically commanded
his subsequent action.


* EOP = Emergency Oversimplification Procedure (See page 25).

In EOP, the mind is extremely conservative of effort.

It is like your overworked assistant
whom you have working three shifts
and you still
(from its viewpoint)
want to shovel more in.

Like anyone who works for somebody else,
the mind in EOP automatically finds the flaws
in new or complicated or difficult work orders —
reasons to change the subject,
put off the new work,
argue for a simpler compromise,
and otherwise avoid impartial consideration
of the proposed new work.


Unlike most assistants, however,
the mind has the ability
(in EOP)
to throw a hypnotic spell over you
which makes you forget the whole idea
and get involved in something else.

The unverbalized words which might be used
to "throw the hypnotic spell" in this case:

*"This stuff is too trivial to think about*
(i.e., I'd be embarrassed if someone was listening) —
*it's simpler*
*just to get to work*
*and forget about it."*

*The sooner one gets boggled
by all the questions sprouting from a chain*

*the sooner one shifts into EOP*

*and "never" learns that chain.*


By generally staying awake
and answering his own questions,

this man will assimilate his experience,
learn, grow, adapt, prosper, evolve.

If he were to generally stay in EOP
and avoid answering his own questions,

they will accumulate,
causing still more EOP,
non-learning,
non-grasping of Life opportunities,
neurosis.


If the man knew this
he would always answer his own questions.

> It might not even have occurred to the man
> to think of this
>
> because he "hasn't got time".

The part of the mind
which makes the decision
to shift into EOP
is notoriously short-sighted.

It cannot weigh a current cost
against a future benefit.

It doesn't think in terms of
"If I always reject questions this way ..."

It merely mechanically reacts
to "this time, now."

> *Imaginations*
> *are clogged*
>
> *with other people's outputs.*
>
> *Key mental work gets avoided.*

If the man was not running in EOP at this point,
something else happens:

the man continues the inner debate
until he gets to the Truth.

In the process of deciding how soon to set to work,
he will also discover
*a few general principles*
which will be extremely valuable to him later on:

These will be general principles about —

- How to resolve such issues

- The evidence of what thoughtless feelings/intuitions tell you

- The evidence of what the universe tells you (phone is not ringing, etc. — universe could be jogging you this way if it wanted)

- The nature of DUTY

- The nature of triviality

This would probably be more valuable to all concerned
than the few extra minutes of "work".

Our implicit cultural assumption, however,
is that this is *not* the case.

## *Let's Look at the Cybernetics of the Situation*

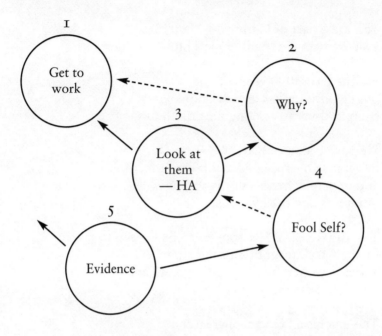

1 — impulse to get to work.

2 — questioned as to motivation.
2 is shown slightly "behind" 1 to suggest *"a wider perspective"*.

3 — looks at 1 & 2, is not attached to the argument.

4 — suggests that the argument be taken seriously.

5 — (unless EOP supervenes) looks at evidence (phone not ringing, what has to get done today, etc.).

6 — decision: contemplate main issues now and write down side issue trigger words, for more extensive contemplation later.

## *A Final Summation*

You are a part of Nature.
You are with it actually One Thing.

For the past 3000 years
our civilization has greatly shifted away
from awareness of being part of Nature.

We have become abstracted from Our Nature
by relative overuse of the thinking function,
and under-awareness of the feelings,
intuitions and the five senses.

This 3000-year trend appears to have been triggered
by the Greek invention of the alphabet,
and accelerated by the printing press and
modern electronic media.

These items all tend to increase
the leftbrain's share of total personal energy,
leading to overuse of verbal/analytical thinking,
and to underuse of (brain core) feelings,
(rightbrain) intuitions
and the (back brain) five physical senses.

On the scale of time
the human race has been around
(about a thousand times longer),
this dramatic shift has just taken place.

One legacy from this historical event pattern
is our current alienation from each other
and from ourselves.

We are alienated because we are unconsciously
filtering out most of our own true Nature,
while we mouth and gesture "acts"
we have picked up in fearful submission
to a rigidly rationalized culture.
We act in conformity with certain thoughts
that have been constantly reinforced in our minds,
while we ignore the inner messages we get
from our feelings and intuitions,
and the outer messages we get from our five senses.


The only way around this today,
with our psychological inheritances being what they are,
is to become conscious of one's own habitual thinking,
feeling, sensing, intuiting and action patterns,
and to start from scratch in reassessing these
and deciding who to be, or rather,
discovering who one is
when one drops the adopted habits of others.

Since you've been reading this book,
you have probably already begun to experience
"leak-throughs" of parts of yourself
that have been buried for years,
but which are now connecting creatively
into various areas of your current life. . .
and parts of yourself that are totally new to you.

This will be an exciting ride.
Your emerging new ways of being
will suggest possible career branchings/spinoffs
whereby more creative and productive use can be made
of the talents and of the ideas you find growing
on your branch of the Tree of Life.


We look forward to hearing from you.

# Pages Especially Useful Under Certain Conditions

Anger  216, 203, 218-220, 76, 213, 224, 230-233, 252, 250

Attachment (*having* to have something come out a certain way, or you can't take it otherwise)  17, 67-68, 72-73, 107-108, 252, 91, 255, 261

Body Problems  250-251, 253, 235-237, 33, 220-221

Coercion  79-80, 115-116, 170, 203, 228, 141, 146-147, 149, 220, 222, 105

Competition  218, 220, 222-223, 224, 226-227, 203, 56, 79, 177, 264

Conflict  203, 206, 208-209, 219-220, 221-224, 226, 233, 14

Dissonance  24, 45-49, 52-57, 203, 164

Divided Self  218, 220, 90, 139, 63-64, 228, 226, 145, 180, 200, 262-264

Fear  252, 211-214, 195, 195-196, 203, 263

Fixation (an unbreakable rut)  242, 76, 140, 143, 194-195, 258, 125, 264

Guilt  69, 193, 90, 92, 194-195, 208-209, 233, 229

Hopelessness  124, 147, 196, 76, 198, 213, 223, 242, 85, 258, 262, 264

Indecisiveness  223, 226, 228, 163-164, 203, 139, 144, 70, 85, 121-122

Information Overload  44, 33, 21-22, 92, 38-39, 27-28, 262-263

Intense Need to Center  250, 238, 173-174, 235-236, 182-184, 185-189, 258, 259

Loneliness   220, 238, 240, 221-222, 232, 263-264

Loss of Sensitivity   250, 232-233, 229, 114, 203, 208-209, 82, 84

Low Self-Esteem   90-92, 66-67, 87-88, 147, 181, 191, 193, 195-196, 198

Narrowing (only allowing a thin slice of you to express itself)   219-223, 233, 213, 132, 47, 55, 76, 76-77, 85, 114-115, 119-120, 264

Non-Forgiveness   232-233, 203, 212-213, 220, 69, 208-209, 227

Non-Trust   220, 222-223, 227, 233, 205, 203, 202-203, 252, 263

Not Knowing   8, 15-16, 85, 110-112, 223, 79, 116-117, 203, 220

Panic   41, 213, 220-221, 192, 195-196, 206, 84, 25, 170, 247

Pressure   248, 247, 41, 43, 241, 25, 24

Seeming Disaster   205, 206, 213, 194-195, 196, 223, 252

Self Enslavement   63-64, 14, 94, 111-112, 155, 71-76, 258, 264

Self Rejection   90-92, 74, 76, 87-88, 146-147, 193, 196, 264

Stagnation   72-76, 77-78, 85, 146-147, 205, 206, 264, 240

Tension   30-32, 33, 250, 253, 170-171, 204, 241, 247

Uselessness   222-223, 90, 125, 196, 220, 258, 191-192, 193, 146-147, 262-263, 264

# Index

Add to Net Value of Universe  17-72, 76-77, 108, 110-111, 175, 226
Advice  13, 14, 231
Approval  56, 57, 87-88, 98-99, 103-110
Attachment  26, 130-131, 252, 255, 261
Attention  45-46, 48, 52, 127, 130, 170, 184, 185, 235-238, 243, 247, 48
Attitude  53, 60, 104, 105, 247
Babbling  56, 243-246
Balance  147-148
Becoming  72, 90-91, 185
Behavior  4, 42, 63, 65, 72-74, 106, 108, 181, 230, 231, 245
Being  40, 78, 100, 149-150, 177, 209, 240
Beliefs  8-11, 13, 17, 67, 71, 76, 94, 116, 117, 154, 159, 163, 203, 222
Biocomputer  25, 29, 32, 60
Body  30, 31, 38, 60, 61, 79, 102, 103, 109, 116, 137-138, 140, 166, 187, 239, 250-253
Brain  6, 7, 20-22, 23, 24, 27, 28, 32, 38, 39, 42, 235, 250, 262
Clarity  27, 31, 33, 133, 238
Closure  24, 40, 45-48, 51, 52, 54, 57, 72, 134, 156, 171, 203
Communication  4, 5, 43, 53, 55, 57, 63, 111, 112, 118, 128, 132, 141, 155, 197, 199, 210, 212 225, 243
Complexity  20, 40, 41, 44, 84
Conscious  14, 21, 27, 38, 40, 46, 30, 62, 68, 70, 179, 184, 185, 239, 243, 263, 218-220, 248
Consciousness  61, 101, 115, 116, 122, 131-134, 150, 178, 184, 207, 217-220, 248
Consistency  71-76, 77, 78, 166, 167
Creativity  43, 62, 76, 81, 83, 147, 166, 206, 232, 264
Cybernetics  19-21, 36
Decisions  12, 17, 23, 24, 25, 31, 44, 46, 64, 66, 112, 137-138, 139, 141, 143, 144, 150, 179, 180, 183, 195-196, 206, 225, 226, 228-229, 248, 259, 260
Desires  72, 73, 90, 104, 106, 163-164, 204, 228, 229, 249
Dissonance  24, 27, 45, 46, 47, 48, 52, 54, 85, 156, 164, 231
Distraction  32, 52, 148, 149, 150, 151, 174, 175, 182, 237, 238, 240
Doing  90, 107-108, 110, 147-148, 196
Doubt  117-118, 161, 167, 169
Emotions  25, 26, 51, 54, 60, 92, 106, 123, 163, 164, 166, 171, 197, 207-208, 214, 215, 218, 246

Energy   1, 17, 125, 193, 195-196, 198, 221-222, 228, 242-246, 253, 262
EOP (Emergency Oversimplification Procedure)   25, 256-261
Evolution   6-7, 17, 67-68, 72-73, 90-91, 205, 223
Expectations   49-55, 81, 91, 194
Fear   211-214, 252
Feelings   10, 11, 13, 36, 37, 45, 61, 65, 74, 75, 85, 90-91, 108, 137-138, 139, 141, 154, 165, 166, 170, 198, 216, 248, 262, 263
Flowing   147-148, 170, 185, 223, 224, 225
Focusing   20, 44, 57, 74, 122-123, 130-132, 133, 175-178, 181, 185, 213
Freedom   48, 169, 247
Future   65-66, 74-76, 101, 124, 196, 205, 229, 247, 249, 259
Gentleness   111-112, 227, 229
Goals   27, 52, 66, 67, 91, 92, 106-112, 145, 147, 148, 151, 194-195, 219, 220, 237
Guilt   69, 193, 246
Gurus   14, 15, 22, 41
Happiness   85, 87, 96, 97, 107, 111, 194, 196, 199
Head Action   130-131, 174, 176-177, 178, 182, 245
Honesty   79, 103-104, 227, 229
Hurrying   49, 135, 142, 143, 147, 163-164
Information   19, 20, 23, 26-29, 34-40, 42, 45, 46, 83, 122-123, 125, 128, 139, 184, 203, 208-209, 228
Input   19-22, 29, 34-35, 75, 149-151, 174, 176-177, 192, 198, 206, 238, 247
Inside   2, 4, 13, 21-22, 30, 43, 63, 68, 74, 75, 90, 94, 101, 111, 112, 114, 115-116, 165, 184
Intuition   118-119, 121-122, 165, 168, 171, 239, 259-260, 262, 263
Judgement   10, 79, 90, 91, 139, 169, 203, 245
Knowing   8, 14, 38-39, 44, 87, 88-89, 94, 109, 111-112, 134, 210
Knowledge   8, 36, 61, 63, 90, 104, 125, 252
Language   2, 8, 55, 116-117
Learning   15, 16, 17, 19-20, 27-28, 44, 71-72, 82, 196, 203, 207-208, 215, 223, 231, 258
Levels   12, 88, 89, 114, 122-123, 128, 140, 181, 237, 239
Life   12, 13, 16, 17, 26, 29, 36, 38, 40, 41, 60, 73, 76, 87-88, 96, 97, 106, 205, 226, 264
Lists   97, 98-99, 100, 101, 163, 169, 242, 247
Love   69, 108, 218, 219
Master   166-169
Master Meditation   182-189
Meditation   25, 27-30, 32, 33, 34-37, 40, 41, 111-112, 118-119, 182-189

Media   19, 20, 22, 23, 34-35
Memory   5, 21, 22, 47, 48, 84, 119, 166, 219, 224-225
Messages   26-28, 31, 38, 39, 87, 111-112, 214, 216, 239, 252, 263
Mind Quiet   170, 171
Moods   42, 60, 114, 160-161, 166, 175, 207-208, 250
Motivations   25, 56-57, 94, 108, 121, 128, 137, 195-196, 200, 201-202, 204, 221-222, 223, 228, 261
Natural Speed   34, 35, 139, 144, 145-147
Nature   29, 34, 238, 251, 262, 263
Negativity   124, 163-164, 171, 197, 198
Non- Rushing   144, 149
Now   17, 40, 73, 76, 90, 91, 98, 113, 117, 118, 121, 138, 139, 142, 143, 247, 248, 251, 259, 264
Objectivity   14, 55, 73, 79, 88, 101, 111, 112, 117, 118, 177
Observation   29, 39, 49, 60, 80, 113-115, 118-125, 228, 250
Observation of Self   64-68, 88, 139, 173-174, 175-176, 177, 183, 230
Oneness   1, 64, 82, 92, 98-99, 102, 111-112, 203, 217-219, 222, 232-233
Overload   19-21, 23, 26, 27-28, 34-35, 38-40, 83
Pain   174-176, 197
Perceptions   1, 5, 45-49, 53, 55, 81, 114, 118-119, 121, 219, 250
Perspective   21-27, 36, 47-48, 65, 79, 85, 121-122, 125, 141, 153, 155, 158, 159-160, 162, 200, 222, 231-232, 238, 261
Positive   84, 144, 198
Pressure   20
Priorities   100, 163-164, 243-244, 247, 253
Problems   29, 163-164, 242
Progress   27-28, 90-91, 92, 107-108, 139, 144-147, 162, 163, 194-195, 220-221, 232, 242
Projects   52, 112, 113, 127, 149, 162, 174, 178, 192, 241
Questions   23, 24, 27, 38, 43, 79, 85, 89, 97, 103-104, 113, 114, 118, 121-122, 124, 139, 155-157, 158-160, 161, 162, 163-164, 228, 229, 256, 258, 261
Rating Oneself   87-92
Reactions   41, 44, 53, 245
Reality   8, 12, 22, 34-35, 49, 53, 88, 114, 116-117, 118, 121-122, 139, 140, 171, 222
Resolutions   74, 75, 157
Robot   29, 43, 88-89, 91-92, 202, 208-209, 220-221, 222, 226, 243-244, 253
Scientific Method   12, 13, 14, 17
Seeing   13, 53, 57, 130-131

Self-Observation  64-68, 88, 139, 173-174, 175, 176, 177, 183, 230
Senate (Senators & Speakers)  65, 153, 156, 157, 158, 160, 162, 165-169
Senses  27, 38, 39, 83, 84, 114, 120, 122-123, 175-176
Situations  30, 39, 40, 43, 170, 171, 181
Society  51-53, 56, 57, 139
Solutions  132-133, 134, 135, 144, 204, 242
Speakers  153-158
Spontaneity  73-78
Subconscious  128, 147-148, 164, 166, 167, 169
Tendencies  11,14, 51, 57, 69, 72, 119-120, 134, 146-147, 230, 253
Tensions  30-32, 33,112, 201, 250, 252, 253
Thinking  45, 47, 56, 60, 63,73, 84, 104, 137-138, 141, 143, 144, 164, 170, 171, 200, 258, 262
Thought Process  15, 23, 36, 37, 43, 46, 47, 57, 67, 71-73, 140, 153, 154, 155, 156, 158, 164, 167, 183, 184, 188, 198, 208-209, 235-236, 262, 263
Time  1,15,23, 24, 31, 52, 125, 132, 133-134, 135, 145, 146, 148-149, 150, 182, 258, 262
Time Pressure  41, 43, 51, 55, 247, 248
Trust  251
Truth  8, 10, 12, 56, 57, 79, 155, 159, 177, 198, 203, 259-260
Understanding  6-7, 14, 24, 43, 45-46, 65, 73, 95, 119, 131, 133, 135, 194, 197, 202, 209, 212, 233, 241
Universe  1,12, 36, 71, 77, 79, 82, 85, 89, 92, 108, 110-112, 122, 128, 165-167, 171, 186, 199, 205, 206, 217-219, 220, 221, 222-225, 226, 227, 230-232, 233, 248, 255, 259-260
Useful Fiction  160, 165, 168
Values  51, 79, 111, 137, 199, 232, 250
Viewpoint  21, 36, 47, 65, 79, 85, 121-122, 125, 141, 153, 155, 158, 159, 162, 200, 222, 232, 238, 261
Visualizing  1, 21, 68, 140, 182, 217-218
Wants  26, 66, 80, 87, 94-112, 137-138, 147-148, 223, 247
Will  29, 43, 94, 104, 111, 149, 160, 161, 168, 196, 209, 213
Words  1-9, 12, 19, 36, 57, 114, 116-117, 124, 130-134, 154, 168, 170, 177-178, 185, 189, 225
Yogis  14, 15, 22, 41